Easter Faith

Easter Faith

BELIEVING IN THE RISEN JESUS

GERALD O'COLLINS, S.J.

PAULIST PRESS
New York/Mahwah, N.J.

Published in the United States in 2003
Paulist Press
997 Macarthur Boulevard
Mahwah, N.J. 07430

Published in Great Britain in 2003
Darton, Longman and Todd Ltd
1 Spencer Court
140–142 Wandsworth High Street
London SW18 4JJ

ISBN 0-8091-4258-9

Designed by Sandie Boccacci
Phototypeset in 12/13pt Perpetua by Intype Libra Ltd
Printed and bound in Great Britain by Page Bros, Norfolk

Contents

CONTENTS

Introduction

SOMETIMES THOSE WHO REVIEW BOOKS on the resurrection of Christ reproach the authors for not having stated precisely what they are writing about, asking, 'Would you please tell us exactly what the resurrection *was*!' The difficulty is that the resurrection cannot be described directly and certainly not exhaustively.

Right from the outset Christians used metaphorical language in speaking about the resurrection. In that event they understood the dead Christ to have been 'woken from the sleep of death' or 'put back on his living feet'. From the time of St Paul they reached for analogies in order to say at least something about an event which is radically, if not totally, different from any other event. The best analogies to the resurrection are the creation of the world (which has happened) and the end of the world (which has not yet happened); those two events point to the transforming power of God at work in raising Jesus – the event which initiates the new creation and constitutes the beginning of the end of all things.

What limits any attempt to clarify the resurrection of Christ comes partly from its 'not yet' character: until resurrection becomes fully a reality for the human race and its world, the resurrection of Christ is not yet completed. Precise clarification of the resurrection is ruled out even more by the fact that it is very closely bound up with our notion of God. In a largely neglected statement, Paul recognised that to be wrong about the resurrection would be to 'misrepresent God' (1 Corinthians 15:15). He held together witness to the resurrection and witness to God. This link made by the Apostle hints at the radical limits in what we can do: any attempt to describe adequately the resurrection would be as misguided as any attempt to describe God adequately.

After those disclaimers let me offer a limited and approximate account of what, on the basis of the New Testament witness and the mainstream tradition of Christianity, I take the resurrection of Jesus to mean. Through a unique divine action which set the ultimate seal of approval on his life and work, Jesus was personally delivered from the state of death. With his earthly body transformed and taken up into a new, glorified existence, he thus initiated the end of all things for human beings and their world (see Romans 8:18–25). Thus his resurrection was primarily 'for him' and secondarily 'for us' (Romans 4:25). Faith in the risen Jesus entails an account like this, even though obviously many believers do not have the biblical and theological training to use such expressions as 'a unique divine action' which sets 'the ultimate seal of approval on the life and work of Jesus'.

This book begins with background theories about God, human beings and the created universe. Those who hold that God created the world but never does anything special now the world is in place have logically ruled out in advance the possibility of Jesus' resurrection from the dead. Hence Chapter 1 critically examines some major views which rule out or rule in the possibility of God raising Jesus from the dead and of Jesus then appearing to those were (or in the case of Paul were to become) his disciples. After this examination of prior theories which can in advance make or unmake Easter faith, Chapter 2 takes up the issue of the historical evidence for the appearances of the risen Jesus and the discovery of his empty tomb. How far does such evidence from history contribute to the making and maintaining of Easter faith? Chapter 3 will argue that the testimony of others and personal experience are decisive in knowing in faith the risen Jesus.

Every now and then some author writes in support of Easter faith and yet throws away, so to speak, the empty tomb script. Chapter 4 addresses the historical case for the reliability of the tradition about Jesus' tomb being discovered open and empty, and moves to reflect on its theological significance. What might the empty tomb indicate about the self-revelation of God and the redemption achieved through the resurrection of the crucified Jesus? Unless they appreciate something of what the empty tomb signifies theologically, believers can find their Easter faith becoming so attenuated that it looks more or less like a belief in the immortality of the soul and no longer in the resurrection of the body, either for Jesus or for themselves. Where Chapter 4 will scrutinise the final chapter of Mark's Gospel, Chapter 5 will attend to the three other Gospels to fill out an account of what the empty tomb tradition, along with other themes in the Easter chapters of Matthew, Luke and John, has to say about the central importance of the resurrection for one's appreciation of the revealing and redeeming activity of the tripersonal God.

The bibliography at the end of this book will (a) list what seem the more useful works I have published on the resurrection and (b) suggest some other reading. I will avoid, as far as possible, repeating what appears under (a). Hence if readers miss what they consider some important point, they may well find it treated in what I have already published.

I am most grateful to several readers of this manuscript – in particular, to Stephen Davis who sent me some very useful criticisms and suggestions. My warm thanks also go out both to the Master of Campion Hall, Fr Gerard J. Hughes, S.J., who honoured me by the invitation to deliver much of this book as the Martin D'Arcy Lectures (October/November 2002), and to those who attended the lectures and improved the text through their comments and questions. Finally, I wish to thank Brendan Walsh, the Editorial Director of Darton, Longman and Todd, who for several years has encouraged me to take up further questions on the resurrection of Jesus.

I dedicate this book to the Jesuits of Campion Hall, both living and dead. Ever since I first came to the United Kingdom in 1965, they have enriched my life by their friendship, hospitality and intellectual challenges.

GERALD O'COLLINS, S.J.
Gregorian University, Rome
New Year's Day 2003

1

Are Background Theories Decisive?

There are more things in heaven and earth,
  Horatio,
Than are dreamt of in your philosophy
                              Hamlet, Act I, Scene V.

SOMETHING CAN BE LEFT OUT when questions about the
resurrection of Jesus are raised. Believers may busy themselves gathering clues in support of their Easter faith. Non-
believers may dismiss out of hand such faith, or else come up
with a diminished version of what the resurrection means: 'Jesus
merely rose in the minds and hearts of his disciples.' In such
exchanges many people may be so full of the particular claims
about the resurrection itself or about such matters as the appearances of the risen Jesus that few will have any time for something
which often implicitly guides their arguments and conclusions:
their foundational beliefs and background theories about God,
human beings, and the material world. In the 1990s a work by
Gerd Luedemann stirred much debate in Germany and, to some
extent, beyond, especially in English-speaking countries.[1] The
book contains not only some insightful comments and criticisms
but also many particular claims that disintegrate on close examination: for instance, the case he makes for arguing that St Paul's
Easter vision was due to his being a genuine hysteric. The deeper
issue, however, does not concern a misguided attempt to specu-
late about Paul's unconscious and write the psycho-biography
of this long-dead figure. What is at stake is Luedemann's

[1]

background theory about the nature of human knowledge. In a 'ruthlessly honest quest for truth', he wants to take 'an undistorted look' at the resurrection, which 'will look in a purely historical and empirical way at the historical context of the testimonies to the resurrection'. Inevitably, those he disagrees with tend to be charged with 'dogmatism', 'prejudice', and even with knowing '*a priori* what needs to be proved'.[2] Luedemann's view of human knowledge exemplifies sadly that naive realism criticised by Bernard Lonergan and others for presuming knowledge to be merely a matter of 'taking an honest look'. The profession of ruthless, undistorted honesty repeats what many scholars have challenged: namely, the claim to make a purely historical, neutral and 'scientific' approach to some controverted issue or person from the past, as if the 'resurrection of Christ' were something 'merely' historical to be kept at arm's length and weighed up dispassionately. But all biblical and historical research takes place on the basis of a whole network of prior judgments and elaborate systems for evaluating and even explaining what is 'real'. There is no such thing as a view from nowhere or presuppositionless research, and it is neither possible nor desirable to undertake such research.[3] Luedemann, however, alleges he is carrying on a totally honest enquiry and is doing something others fail to do: he looks without any bias at the evidence or rather at the evidence which he allows to count. Any debate with him should begin with his flawed background theories about knowledge in general and historical knowledge in particular. His conclusions about the resurrection seem predetermined by some philosophical (and, as we shall see, by some theological) presuppositions which he brings to the issue of the resurrection. These presuppositions have fatally narrowed his vision of what might be accepted about the fate of Jesus.

After this cautionary tale, I want to examine several background theories which influence the way people reflect on and even reject out of hand claims about the resurrection of Jesus. Often such theories are unquestioned, secret presences in the argument; occasionally they are blatantly acknowledged. Let us begin with God and the divine activity in the created world.

God, Divine Action and Faith

Some writers on Christ's resurrection come to this specific question having already decided that, whatever it means, it cannot mean that God acted in a special way to raise the dead Jesus to a new, transformed existence. Having created the universe with its physical laws, God always respects those laws and never acts in ways which suspend or override them. Hence such writers, like the classical Deists of the seventeenth and eighteenth centuries, when discussing miraculous deeds reported by the New Testament, either dismiss them as legendary accretions which appeal only to the credulous and not to those of 'good sense', or interpret them in ways which omit any special divine activity. Such a mindset could never accept that the tomb of Jesus was found to be empty because God had raised the dead Jesus to a final life of glory.[4] 'The scientific picture of the world' endorsed by Luedemann, for instance, excludes the miraculous and rules out in advance the possibility of a unique divine action which brought about Jesus' rising from the tomb.[5]

But should one accept such a 'ban' on special divine activity and view the universe as a closed continuum of causes and effects over which God exercises no control? Does this ban come from a deeply flawed philosophy about the world as a rigidly uniform system – from 'scientism' rather than from science? Is such a view compatible with faith in an all-powerful, omnipresent God who acts with perfect freedom and love? The God from whom the created world, its laws and their operations depend from moment to moment can presumably override at times such laws for very good reasons which may not, or may not yet, be clear to us. While usually respecting the natural order of the world and its functioning (and so not indulging in frequent exceptions to the laws of creation), God is not blocked from performing such special and even unique actions as that of raising Jesus from the dead. In this case, God acts in ways that are qualitatively distinct and different from the ordinary divine 'work' in creating and sustaining the world.

Some want to reduce this picture of God by abandoning, for instance, the divine omnipotence. Faced with death, God cannot make things any different and offer Jesus or anyone else a new and glorious life for ever. Thus A. J. M. Wedderburn ends his examination of the resurrection by suspending judgment about its factuality and meaning. He remains firmly agnostic about the post-resurrection appearances, the historicity of the empty tomb, the new life of Jesus, and the final resurrection for his followers. He concludes with a picture of Jesus having offered his life to God and invites us to do the same; we should embrace a vulnerable, this-worldly faith and life modelled on the example of Jesus.[6] It is Wedderburn's picture of God which seems to control what he is willing or unwilling to share with Paul, John, and the other New Testament witnesses to the resurrection. Any fruitful debate with Wedderburn would have to address itself to his theological and philosophical presuppositions about God before examining his particular pieces of exegesis. Can God fail to be omnipotent and remain God?[7]

Like some others, Wedderburn also seems to share a presupposition about faith and its lack of support which helps to decide his agnostic position on the resurrection. He praises 'the vulnerability of a faith that does not find the protection of firm proofs of its validity in the resurrection stories'.[8] It seems as if any legitimising of faith through God's victory over death would tamper with the purity of an unprotected faith. The fewer the reasons, the more genuine the faith?

Over thirty years ago such theological convictions about faith seemed to control the way in which Willi Marxsen argued biblically about the resurrection. Faith is simply a venture, a commitment made in answer to a call. Any alleged legitimation of Jesus' claims through the event of the resurrection would be incompatible with this venture. It is not just that faith goes beyond the evidence; it excludes evidence. Any rational appeal would distort faith. To believe because we accepted the testimony of those witnesses who met Jesus gloriously alive after his death would render impossible a trusting commitment to Jesus' challenge.[9]

Wedderburn and Marxsen converge in championing a vulnerable, unsupported faith, which partly predetermines their views of the resurrection. Marxsen, however, elaborates more clearly a closely connected and relevant presupposition: about the historian and the believer. From the outset, Marxsen resolutely holds apart matters of information and the call to faith. The historian deals with matters of information and alone has the task of deciding whether some alleged past event really happened. According to Marxsen, 'The historian's answer to the question of whether Jesus rose from the dead must be: "I do not know; I am no longer able to discover." ' Even if historians were able to answer this question positively, such 'isolated talk about the reality of Jesus' resurrection' would constitute a statement apart from faith and remain simply 'the report of a somewhat unusual event'.[10] We meet here a sharp distinction between the historian and the believer, what many see as an unwarranted separation of the cognitive side of faith from the decision to commit oneself – a radical isolation of faith from (historical) reason. This separation glosses over the fact that historians can be believers (or non-believers); in these cases the same individuals think and believe (or disbelieve). Such people would not be flattered to be described as 'schizophrenic' thinkers, as if their belief (or non-belief) were radically separated from their historical reason and knowledge.

The Search for Analogies

So far we have examined some background theories which can decide what some authors think was possible or impossible about the fate of the crucified Jesus: theories about allegedly 'neutral' historical knowledge, about God being unwilling or even unable to override the laws of the created universe, and about faith being independent of and even excluding any reliable historical information. Some other background theories bear directly on *analogies*, both analogies to Jesus' risen life and to the primary way in which the New Testament witnesses claim to have known Jesus' resurrection: namely, his post-resurrection appearances.

Certain authors apparently share a wide-spread modern 'faith' or background theory that it is in principle possible to account for any occurrences 'scientifically', no matter how extraordinary they seem, by finding some close analogies. There can be nothing genuinely new under the sun; allegedly unique events can always be explained by relating them to our existing body of knowledge. Thus the Easter appearances to Mary Magdalene, Peter, Paul, and the other witnesses, reported by the New Testament, can be subsumed under general 'laws' about bereavement experiences, mystical experiences and so forth. This is to blunt anything special, let alone anything uniquely once-and-for-all, about those appearances and the event they allegedly revealed: Christ's resurrection from the dead. Before inspecting particular analogies and the way in which they function as background theories, let me say something about analogy in general.

Those who value analogies look for significant likenesses between events, objects or persons. Their act of comparing may let them detect many similarities or perhaps only a few; the similarities they observe may be close or very remote. The similarities between two plants, for instance, may be so close and numerous that botanists will decide that they are in fact dealing with an identical species. Or else some proposed analogy – let us say between a tortoise and a playing field, because both slope up in the middle – may be so slight and remote that it does not prove to be illuminating in any serious way either about tortoises or about playing fields. Tortoises are living, small, and (relatively) mobile; playing fields are dead (even if they normally host live grass and worms), large, and do not move. On the scale of 'like–unlike' the analogy between objects or events may come anywhere between the two extremes. A merely remote analogy will hardly help our understanding and interpretation. It certainly should not support misguided attempts at an argument from analogy. We cannot maintain that because X (let us say the tortoise) is like Y (the playing field) in one respect (or even in several respects), therefore the tortoise and the playing field must also be similar in other respects. In fact, the argument from analogy does not work even with close analogies: from the existence of a number of close similarities we cannot logically conclude that the two objects or events must therefore be similar in some other respects.

Appropriate analogies do not function by proving something or by adding to our knowledge things which we did not previously know or would not otherwise have known. Rather, through evoking things we already know and relating new information to our prior knowledge and beliefs, illuminating analogies can yield insights into fresh data which we have acquired or lend a certain plausibility to claims, perhaps strikingly unusual claims, that others are making. Analogies function to 'place', and perhaps generalise, the new data that come along.

Given the way some have misused the principle of analogy, it is important to remark that analogies should not produce a one-sided orientation towards typical events at the expense of unusual or even unique claims. By dealing with what is similar but not identical, analogy allows for what is dissimilar and different, even strikingly different, and does not unilaterally suppress the new. Analogy, by looking for some measure of likeness but not straight identity, makes plenty of room for novelty, and allows us to appreciate what is new by relating it to what is old and familiar. But appeal to analogies does not justify denying or simply excluding in principle the possibility of the strikingly unfamiliar or even of the genuinely new.[11]

Analogies to the Resurrection

In the case of Jesus' resurrection from the dead, analogies have been operating ever since Christians began proclaiming their message. The resurrection could not be totally new and utterly without analogy. Otherwise neither the first Christians nor anyone else could grasp it or say anything at all about it. In fact, right from the start natural, biblical and sacramental analogies began to operate. Let us recall, first of all, some analogies taken from ordinary human experience of the created world.

The very verbs which the first Christians consistently employed in their Easter message incorporated analogies. By using *egeiro*, they maintained that what had happened to Jesus was like someone being woken from the sleep of death. By using *anistemi*, they spoke of him being put back on his (living) feet. A natural analogy was built into these two verbs which the New Testament applied to the resurrection of Jesus and that of others. The way was prepared for other analogies, which – encouraged by the example of Paul in 1 Corinthians 15:35–44 (and John 12:24) – Church writers were to take from the fecundity of the natural world. Seed is sown in the earth and plants sprout up; night falls and a new day dawns; after the death of winter, there comes the fresh life of spring. The wonder of pregnancy and birth prompted Paul and other early Christians to adopt another comparison: the risen Christ is the 'first-born' from the dead (e.g. Romans 8:29; Colossians 1:18). All these analogies were, however, qualified by the belief that the resurrection of Christ was a definitive, once-and-for-all event of transformation and therefore much more than a remarkably striking example from some repeated occurrences in the created world like harvests, the change of seasons, and the birth of children.[12]

Then there are the biblical analogies. One can apply the words of the Book of Wisdom, 'from the greatness and beauty of created things comes a corresponding perception of their creator' (13:5), to the new creation. First of all comes the analogy between the resurrection as new creation and the original creation story in Genesis 1—2. When Paul developed his theme of the crucified and risen Christ as 'the last Adam' (1 Corinthians 15:20–23, 45–49), he compared and contrasted 'the first man' (Adam) with 'the second man' (Christ). Here and later in Romans 5, the Apostle was at pains to highlight the dissimilarities between the two collective figures: between the first who brought death and the second who brought life. Nevertheless, the comparison entailed some similarities – between the original creation and the new creation of resurrection. In creating the material world, with Adam and Eve as its high point, God called into existence what had not yet existed. In re-creating the world through resurrection, God calls to a new existence what has existed but is now dead. The contrast between the first Adam and the last Adam thus involves a certain analogy between the first creation and the new creation of resurrection.

Second, the fact that the crucifixion and resurrection occurred at the time of the Passover naturally encouraged believers to see a similarity between the Jewish people's liberation from Egypt and Jesus' liberation from death. God's glory was revealed in both acts of deliverance. The original exodus and its various details inspired and furthered Christian understanding and interpretation of Jesus' exodus from death to resurrection (e.g. 1 Corinthians 5:7). The first exodus was not invoked to prove the resurrection but to elucidate it and share in it more deeply.

The author of the Letter to the Hebrews drew a third, detailed analogy for Jesus' death and entrance into the heavenly sanctuary from the yearly Day of Expiation or *Yom Kippur*. This anonymous author elaborated the similarities which bore on such matters as the conditions for priesthood, the terminology of sacrifice, and the place of the priestly functions. At the same time, he stressed the dissimilarities between Jesus' priesthood and that of the Levitical priests. The once-and-for-all nature of the priestly deed accomplished in the death and resurrection of the Son of God made this case strikingly different. The complex analogy at the heart of the Letter to the Hebrews works very well both through likeness and unlikeness. Where this analogy arose on the basis of something familiar that happened year by year on a particular day, the exodus analogy recalled a once-and-for-all event in the history of God's people.

By extending Jesus' saying about Jonah and his preaching to the Ninevites (Luke 11:29–30, 32), Matthew found a fourth analogy in another single and unrepeated episode, this time from a quite legendary story. The evangelist took the sign of Jonah to include the prophet's being three days and three nights inside the sea monster and to form an analogy to the Son of Man being three days and three nights in the bowels of the earth (Matthew 12:39–41). The biblical record thus provided analogies for Jesus' resurrection that came from the creation story of Genesis, a shadowy but foundational event in the story of God's people (the exodus), the yearly ceremony of *Yom Kippur*, and a vivid, extended parable (featuring the adventures of Jonah).

Matthew's development of the Jonah analogy has enjoyed a long influence in art; from the time of early paintings in the catacombs, Christian artists have followed suit and continued to find an edifying likeness between the story of Jonah's adventure and Jesus' death, burial and deliverance from the grave. Christian art and literature have also found analogical precedents to the resurrection in such biblical stories as those of Noah and his family being delivered from the flood, Daniel from the lion's den, the three youths from the fiery furnace, and Susannah from the two wicked elders. Yet the exodus story remained *the* analogical prototype of Jesus' deliverance that brought human redemption. Christian liturgies reflect the centrality of this analogy in many ways: for instance, in taking over for Holy Saturday two songs with which Moses and Miriam led the people in praising God for their liberation from slavery.

Alongside natural and biblical analogies to Jesus' resurrection from the dead, from the outset Christians have employed sacramental analogies. Baptism and the eucharist, in particular, illuminate and are illuminated by the events of the first Good Friday and Easter Sunday. From the beginning of Christianity believers understood their once-and-for-all act of being baptised to re-enact through sacramental signs the redemptive death, burial and resurrection of Jesus. In dying and being buried with Christ, the baptised are freed from sin and rise to new life (Romans 6:1–11; Colossians 2:12–13). This sacramental analogy is both like and unlike the resurrection of Jesus. He was literally buried and then delivered from the grave, whereas in the case of baptism the language of 'being buried' and 'being delivered' from the waters is used in an extended sense. Baptism does not normally bring a literal death and burial to those being baptised. In *The Violent Bear it Away* Flannery O'Connor tells the story of a dim-witted child who is simultaneously baptised and drowned in a lake. But this linking of baptism and literal death, while carrying forward her novel and its message, is meant to be bizarre and not a normal case in point.

The repeated celebration of the eucharist puts Christians into a situation that recalls and is analogous to the dying and rising of Jesus. As St Paul expressed matters, the eucharist means 'announcing the death of the (risen) Lord until he comes' (1 Corinthians 11:26). Thus through once-and-for-all rites (baptism) and in repeated ceremonies (the eucharist), Christian sacraments from the beginning have yielded analogies to Jesus' resurrection from the dead.

To sum up: from the beginning of Christianity natural, biblical and sacramental analogies have been pressed into service to illuminate the fate of Jesus. The natural and biblical analogies contributed to the 'background theories' which supported and clarified faith in the resurrection for the first disciples, both those who claimed to have seen the risen Jesus and those to whom they preached the Easter message. At once they began to baptise and celebrate the eucharist, rites which both had deep roots in Jewish history and practice and gave ongoing support to faith in the risen Jesus. In this way we can rightly locate the analogies drawn from nature, the scriptures and the emerging sacramental life of Christianity as shaping the background theories which early Christians brought to their acceptance of the resurrection.

Bereavement Experiences

In the next chapter we will examine more closely the appearances of the risen Christ reported by the New Testament. The classic list of six such appearances (to three individuals and to three groups), which comes from St Paul (1 Corinthians 15:5–8), offers very little information about what is claimed to have happened; even the Easter narratives in the Gospels and Acts 1 remain very sketchy. Is there any chance of filling out the picture by appealing to analogies?

From what we read about the appearances of the risen Jesus to Mary Magdalene, Peter, Paul and others, can we glean, for example, some underlying structure which will justify aligning this New Testament witness with experiences which bereaved people frequently have of their dead partners?[13] Are there closely similar patterns between the Easter appearances and the experiences of meeting deceased loved ones reported by bereaved people? On closer examination this proposed analogy proves remote and inappropriate and hence fails to prove illuminating in any serious way. Let us see the details.

In a pioneering study, 'The Hallucinations of Widowhood',

W. Dewi Rees drew together the findings from his investigation of 227 widows and 66 widowers.[14] He reported that 46.7 per cent of the 293 persons interviewed claimed to have experienced their beloved dead at variable times during the day; dreams were not considered in the study. The bereaved had 'felt the presence of' the deceased (39.2 per cent), 'seen' them (14 per cent), 'heard' them (13.3 per cent), 'spoken' to them (11.6 per cent) and, very occasionally, been 'touched' by them (2.7 per cent). Some of the widows and widowers interviewed reported having had more than one type of experience; and in 36.1 per cent of all the cases these experiences of the beloved dead lasted for many years.

Rees called these experiences 'hallucinations', a word that the 1996 edition of the *Encyclopedia Americana* defines as a 'report of a sensory experience in the absence of an actually external stimulus appropriate to the reported experience'. The same entry in that encyclopedia goes on to remark that hallucinations are 'very commonly reported' among mental patients, and that 'normal persons suffering from extreme fatigue' or sensory deprivation (e.g. in laboratory experiments) may experience hallucinations. Other scholars use milder language than Rees: Andrew Greeley entitled a chapter of a book on religious experience 'Religious Stories and Contact with the Dead'.[15] Rees' use of 'hallucinations' implies a negative evaluation of the experiences he reports and stands in some tension with the fact that none of his cases involved mental patients, extreme fatigue or sensory deprivation. While 17.7 per cent of those he investigated suffered some depression which required medical treatment after their bereavement, 68.6 per cent were 'helped by their hallucinations', and a further 25.5 per cent 'found them neither helpful nor unpleasant' (p. 40). Rees concluded from his study that 'hallucinations are normal experiences after widowhood' (p. 41).

Admittedly, we can make some comparisons between the experiences of Rees' widows and widowers and those of the first disciples after Jesus' death and burial. In both cases we learn of contact with the beloved dead, and it is a contact that is or at least can be helpful and life-giving. Beyond that, detailed comparison shows up serious differences. To begin with, Jesus' first disciples remembered him as having made extraordinary public claims about his identity and mission before dying a horrible and utterly shameful death on a public scaffold. Rees reports no cases of anything like that among his 293 widows and widowers. Apropos of the place of their spouses' death, 270 out of 293 either died at home (161 cases) or in hospital (109 cases). The cases examined by Rees do not parallel what the New Testament has to report about the personal claims of Jesus, his terrible death and the situation of his disciples. Then other reasons suggest that the analogy is not close or illuminating.

The widows and widowers studied by Rees were all *individuals* who 'felt the presence of', 'saw', 'heard', 'spoke to' or were 'touched by' their dead spouses. Around 40 per cent of them continued to do so for many years. Only 27.7 per cent of them, prior to Rees' study, had mentioned their experiences to others; the rest had not disclosed their experiences, even to close friends and relatives. None of those whose bereavement experiences are reported by Rees dramatically changed their lifestyle and became missionaries proclaiming to the world their experience and what it implied. All these points move the bereavement analogy away from the situation of Jesus' disciples. In their case groups such as 'the Twelve' and 'more than five hundred' (1 Corinthians 15:5, 6), and not just individuals, were remembered as having seen Jesus. The encounters with the groups and the individuals did not continue for many years.[16] Those to whom Jesus appeared quickly passed on this good news to others; they did not keep this experience to themselves, as did 72.3 per cent of the cases investigated by Rees. From what we know of some disciples such as Peter and Paul, it was not simply that they told others of their new experiences; their lives changed dramatically and they became missionary witnesses to the crucified and risen Jesus. In short, there are many serious differences between the case of the bereaved and that of Jesus' disciples – differences that may not be ignored or cancelled with a wave of the hand. We misrepresent matters if we allege a close and illuminating analogy.

In the years that followed Rees' pioneering work, Colin Murray Parkes contributed much in the field of bereavement research. One of his collaborative studies is cited by Luedemann;[17] it is a 1983 study of the grief experiences of 49 widows and 19 widowers. It is important to note that the spouses of these widows and widowers *all* died from natural causes or from accidents. Cases involving spouses who had died from suicide or homicide (not to mention execution) were deliberately excluded from the study. In a later work, *Bereavement Studies of Grief in Adult Life*,[18] Parkes dedicates a few pages (pp. 60–65) to the 'searching' and 'finding' through which bereaved persons may seek to mitigate the pain of grieving and so enjoy a 'sense of presence' and a 'bereavement dream' of the deceased. Even if he will not use the loaded term 'hallucination', Parkes writes of the one who is being sought as 'absent' and concludes by saying: 'No matter how happy the dream, there must always be a "sad awakening" ' (p. 65). It is worth pointing out that the resurrection traditions in the New Testament never mention any such 'sad awakening' for those men and women credited with having seen Jesus gloriously alive after his death.

In examining background theories some bring to their reflections on the post-resurrection appearances of Jesus, we have reported and evaluated one (recent) example of such theories: the experiences of bereavement. We concluded that the experiences of bereaved persons do not closely and directly parallel the Easter appearances reported by the New Testament. The testimony to those appearances is not illuminated by the research published by Dewi Rees, Colin Murray Parkes and others.

Luedemann, however, appeals to such research in fashioning an updated version of the thesis advanced in 1835 by David Friedrich Strauss: that the post-resurrection appearances were merely internal, psychological events which took place totally in the minds of the first disciples and were not produced by any extra-subjective source. In short, those 'appearances' were purely subjective visions, with no external reality corresponding to them – what Luedemann calls 'hallucinations' which can be totally explained by the psychology of the process of mourning.[19] His background theory about the psychology of mourning excludes in principle anything genuinely new in the Easter appearances. They are no more than ancient examples in the psycho-biography of some bereaved persons.

Let us now consider an analogy such earlier writers as Adolf Deissmann (d. 1937), Rudolf Otto (d. 1937), Albert Schweitzer (d. 1965) and Evelyn Underhill (d. 1941) have suggested in various ways: a comparison between mystical visions and the Easter experiences. Some of these writers approached the issue out of their background in biblical studies of St Paul (e.g. Deissmann and Schweitzer); others (e.g. Underhill) took up the question in the context of her study of prayer, mystical and otherwise.[20]

Mystical Visions

Those who have tried to press the analogy with bereavement experiences can be agnostic about the existence of God and eternal life after death. Even if they evaluate positively what the widows and widowers under study may experience for some years, the experiences may be readily assessed in merely human and this-worldly terms. Those earlier writers, however, who explored the Easter experiences in the light of their knowledge about mystical visions almost inevitably built God and the after-life into their analogy. So, far from these visions being mere hallucinations, they open, so to speak, a 'window on heaven' and put the mystics in close touch with God. Moreover, far from this analogy being reductive, it can allow for what was strikingly new and even unique about the post-resurrection appearances.

The name 'mystical' is given to:

(a) deeply personal, often intense experiences of the direct and immediate presence of God, which

(b) are received rather than achieved by 'mystics',

(c) bring them some special knowledge of and communion with God,

(d) radically change their style of life,

(e) are associated with some 'dark night' of suffering, and

(f) stimulate them to love and serve others.[21]

Every item in this working definition is controversial, can be debated, invites long explanations, and may not be true of all examples of mystical experiences, both within Christianity and beyond. For instance, claims to a direct or 'immediate' contact with God, as in (a), call for qualification. Any 'immediate' presence of God is always, as experts in the field of mysticism convincingly argue, 'mediated' in one way or another. Then (b) may be questioned: can we speak about 'acquired' mysticism or are such experiences always received as strikingly free gifts from God? As regards (d), obviously some mystics have already undergone a radical conversion of life before they receive particular mystical experiences. Such experiences will serve to confirm and encourage a change in lifestyle which has already occurred. But, if we set aside the debates and qualifications, can we, for instance, accept at least a *prima facie* case for recognising how the six points are verified in the case of one Easter witness, St Paul? Let us test the hypothesis by taking up what Paul himself has to say about his Damascus Road encounter and subsequent life and bracket off the later accounts offered by Luke in the Acts of the Apostles (in chapters 9, 22, and 26).

Although he is not interested in describing in detail his encounter with the risen Lord or what he received in 'a revelation of Jesus Christ' (Galatians 1:12), Paul has this to say in his Letter to the Galatians:

> You have heard, no doubt, of my earlier life in Judaism. I was violently persecuting the church of God and was trying to destroy it. I advanced in Judaism beyond many among my people of the same age, for I was far more zealous for the traditions of my ancestors. But when God, who had set me apart before I was born and called me through his grace, was pleased to reveal his Son to me, so that I might proclaim him among the Gentiles, I did not confer with any human being . . . Then [after some years] I went into the regions of Syria and Cilicia, and I was still unknown by sight to the churches of Judea that are in Christ; they only heard it said, 'The one who formerly

was persecuting us is now proclaiming the faith he once
tried to destroy.'

(Galatians 1:13–16, 21–23, NRSV)

A number of things which Paul says here can be lined up with
features in our working definition of mysticism.

Paul seems to talk about (a) a direct contact with God who
'revealed his Son' to him, or as he puts it in terms of the Son's
action: 'he appeared also to me' (1 Corinthians 15:8). Some commentators on Galatians write of an 'ecstatic' experience of the
divine presence in the Damascus Road encounter, but neither in
Galatians nor elsewhere does Paul write in those terms of that
encounter.[22] However, as experts on mysticism normally agree,
ecstasy, trances and other such phenomena do not belong essentially to mystical experiences. Second, the sovereign freedom of
God (b) characterises what happened to Paul. The 'revelation'
of the Son took place when it 'pleased' God, who had already
'set apart' Paul before birth and 'called' him through the divine
'grace'. The apostle expresses the grace he received in his
encounter with Christ and its aftermath by saying that 'he took
hold of me' (Philippians 3:12). As regards the third characteristic
of mystical experiences, (c), Paul records 'the sublime knowledge of Christ Jesus my Lord' (Philippians 3:8) with which he
had been gifted. It was and is a knowing which goes beyond the
standards of ordinary human knowledge (2 Corinthians 5:16).
The gift of this special knowledge initiated an intimate and
enduring fellowship with the glorious Christ, Paul's intense
feeling of belonging 'in Christ' and living a total communion of
life: 'It is no longer I who live, but it is Christ who lives in me'
(Galatians 2:20).

Then the last three items in our working definition of mysticism look as if they too are verified in what Paul says about
himself. The influence of Paul's Damascus Road encounter shows
through the radical change in his life (d). The man who had been
'violently persecuting the church of God and trying to destroy
it', to the amazement of Christians in Judea, had turned around
completely. He was 'now proclaiming the faith he once tried to

destroy'. The mystical encounter changed a persecutor into an apostle. The dark night of suffering, (e), with naked faith and vulnerable love, featured in Paul's repeated account of the painful experiences which followed his dramatic call when Christ 'took hold of him' for his apostolic ministry (2 Corinthians 4:8–12; 6:4–10; 11:23–33; 12:7–10). That suffering came as the aftermath of his original, mystical experience. Finally, as for (f), so far from that experience alienating him from other human beings, Paul, like all authentic mystics, turned to them with outstandingly generous love (1 Corinthians 15:8–10). He spoke of the paternal (1 Corinthians 4:15; 1 Thessalonians 2:11) and maternal (Galatians 4:19; 1 Thessalonians 2:7) tenderness which characterised his work for them.

Thus a possibility emerges for drawing some parallels between mystical experiences of a visionary kind and what one New Testament witness (Paul) has to say about his encounter with the risen Christ. But Karl Rahner rightly warns against pressing the analogy and likening the Easter experience of the disciples 'too closely to mystical visions of an imaginative kind'. He stresses the 'peculiar nature' of the Easter experience and even talks about it as 'an experience which is strictly *sui generis*'. Among his reasons for not pressing the analogy, Rahner points out that the Easter experience is 'reserved to a definite phase in salvation history' and 'bestows' on the Easter witnesses 'a unique task'.[23]

As happens often enough in his theological writing, Rahner does not cite any particular biblical evidence in support of his argument. But presumably he has in mind such passages as 1 Corinthians 15:8 ('last of all he appeared also to me') and John 20:29 (which implies that only the Easter witnesses 'saw and believed', whereas all later disciples would be called to believe, even though they had never had the experience of 'seeing'). Whatever the specific details of the appearances to Peter, Mary Magdalene, Paul and the other basic witnesses, those experiences ended. Thus the New Testament witness supports the conclusion that the post-resurrection encounters with the risen Christ were, both in fact and in principle, limited to certain individuals and groups at the start of the Christian movement. This significant difference between the original Easter experiences and later Christian experiences of the risen Lord is associated with the 'unique task' of the Easter witnesses as authoritative founders of the Church, a task for a specific stage in salvation history and one which no later generation could fully share.[24] The once-and-for-all task of the apostolic founders clearly implies for Rahner something special, unrepeatable or even unique about the Easter experience on which that task rested (see 1 Corinthians 9:1). Hence, he argues that experience should not be likened simply and completely to mystical experiences which we find elsewhere.

One might probe the strength of this argument. We could – and, I would hold, should – agree that the apostolic founders of the Church received a special, even unique mission, which involved an irreplaceable function for the subsequent history of the Church. But does such a mission imply that there also had to be something special and even unique about the key experience (an appearance of the risen Christ) that played a decisive role in conferring such a once-and-for-all mission? Do we expect and how would we justify expecting such a connection between the mission and the experience which gave rise to it? A case for justifying such a connection could, I think, be cautiously mounted by examining what we know from the whole sweep of salvation history, from the story of Abraham, the prophets, and key figures in the New Testament and beyond. Consistently there seems to be some kind of link between their foundational experience and subsequent mission. Undoubtedly in many cases we seem to know much more about their mission (the public effect) than about the cause which triggered it (for instance, the call of an Old Testament prophet or the experience of Jesus at his baptism). Nevertheless, a special mission appears to presuppose an experience, which others at the time or later do not share or do not fully share.

Rahner also claims that the first disciples, while conscious that the Easter experience of the risen Christ was 'given from without' and not 'produced' by themselves, were also aware that it was 'different' from visionary experiences which were 'familiar' to them.[25] Once again Rahner cites no texts, but once again he has ample backing from the New Testament. It presents a fairly wide range of visionary experiences, but reports the Easter appearances quite differently. Unlike the angelic communications to Joseph (Matthew 1:20–21; 2:13, 19–20), none of the Easter appearances is said to occur in a dream during sleep. With the possible exception of John 20:19, they do not take place by night, as do several 'revelations' mentioned in Acts (16:9–10; 18:9; 23:11; 27:23–24). Nor can these appearances be likened to Peter's vision of the sheet let down from heaven. Even though that experience occurs by day and when he is awake, unlike the Easter appearances it happens in ecstasy (Acts 10:9–16). To sum up, the New Testament, while calling certain phenomena 'visions' (Luke 24:23; 2 Corinthians 12:1),[26] does not use this term of a resurrection appearance except in one passage (Acts 26:19). What is more important than terminology, however, is the fact that, except in Luke's three versions of the Damascus Road encounter, we would never consider classifying the post-resurrection appearances as mystical visions of a 'familiar' kind. In reality, when Luke tells the story of the encounter, a light flashes around Paul who hears a voice which identifies itself as that of Jesus (Acts 9:3–8; 22:6–11; 26:12–18). Despite Acts 9:17 and 26:16, 19, Paul, as Luke tells the story, does not see Jesus in a vision or appearance. Of course, one must be cautious in talking about what the first disciples were 'conscious' of and 'familiar' with. Nevertheless, the fact remains that the New Testament recalls the post-resurrection appearances as if they were 'different' from various visionary and ecstatic experiences it mentions elsewhere. The appearances ended, while the latter experiences (e.g. Acts 10:9–16, 44–46; 27:23–24; Revelation 1:10–20) continued. Rahner seems correct in making this point in support of his general case that the Easter appearances differ significantly from mystical visions of an imaginative kind.

What Rahner should also have remarked is that the New Testament reports Easter appearances not only to single individuals but also to groups, in particular 'the Twelve' (e.g. 1 Corinthians 15:5) and the five hundred (1 Corinthians 15:6). Accounts of the visions of Teresa of Avila, John of the Cross, and other mystics, which might be considered to parallel the post-resurrection appearances to Peter, Mary Magdalene, Paul, and others, can be cited. But such mystical visions can hardly be used to interpret the appearances to groups of disciples and their collective, perceptual experiences of the risen Christ.

Moving from the New Testament and its record of the special experiences and tasks involved in founding the Church, Rahner draws on Christian theology and its evaluations. He adds a further consideration which sets the appearances of the risen Christ apart from the visions of Teresa of Avila, John of the Cross and other such classical mystics. 'The theology of mysticism,' he writes, 'denies to the mystics to whom Jesus "appears" the character of being resurrection witnesses, and denies to their visions any equality with the appearances of the risen Christ to the apostles.' 'Our faith' in the risen Christ 'remains tied to the apostolic witnesses.'[27] In the history of Christianity the great mystics have attracted much attention as teachers of prayer and leaders of religious reform. But neither they themselves nor their leading commentators have ever tried to legitimate their function by claiming that mystics take their place with the first disciples in witnessing to the truth of Christ's resurrection from the dead. Any visions which mystics enjoyed of the risen Christ may confirm for some or even many people his loving presence within the Church and beyond. But no mainstream Christian thinker that I know of suggests that those visions offer the foundational validation for Easter faith which 'comes to us' (First Eucharistic Prayer) from the apostolic witnesses. These visions do not belong to the experience of foundational 'revelation' (Galatians 1:12, 16) which reached its climax with the death and resurrection of Jesus, along with the coming of the Holy Spirit.

Christic Visions
Let me explore briefly a further possible analogy: contemporary visions of Jesus. Precisely because they came from living persons whom he could interview, Phillip Wiebe studied 28 cases (11 men and 17 women) who reported having visions of the risen

Christ.[28] He wished to explore whether these 'contemporary experiences bear any similarity to those that seem to lie behind the New Testament accounts of post-Resurrection appearances of Jesus'.[29] Those he interviewed reported visions of Jesus which happened in a great variety of circumstances (in settings that included not only 'church' worship but also a wide range of everyday contexts), to those who reported various affiliations (Anglican, Catholic, Greek Orthodox, Methodist, other Protestant denominations, and some not attached to any particular Christian community), in many places (in Australia, Canada, England, the United States, and Wales), and to people of different ages (from 14 to 91 years of age at the time of their vision(s).

These contemporary visions of Jesus seemed to share some characteristics of the original Easter appearances:

(a) the onset, duration, and content of their visions of Jesus were neither initiated nor controlled by the percipients, just as the Easter appearances seem to have been entirely dependent on the initiative of the risen Jesus;

(b) many of the visions are reported to have taken place in a normal physical environment, just as did the Easter appearances reported by Matthew, Luke and John;

(c) frequently the percipients of visions were passing through periods of pain and suffering when the vision of Jesus happened (see, for example, cases 3, 4, 5, 6, 10, 11, and 13), as was the case with the disciples who followed Jesus and then saw his mission come to a horrible end of the cross.

But then there were the differences, which Wiebe recalls: in particular, the way in which the percipients of the Christic visions immediately and confidently identified the figure in their visions as Jesus himself. This feature sets these visions apart from Luke 24:13–31, 36–43, John 20:14–15 and 21:4, and Matthew 28:17, which indicate that the disciples had initial hesitations about the One they were encountering or even failed to recognise him for some time. Add too the glorious radiance which the percipients of Christic visions repeatedly report and which is notably absent from the New Testament encounters with the risen Christ, apart from Luke's three accounts of Paul's experience on the Damascus Road (Acts 9, 22, 26). Wiebe is understandably prudent about pushing the analogy between the Christic visions and the post-resurrection appearances, and does something which others who look for analogies repeatedly fail to do. He draws attention both to the similarities and the differences. At the end, he wisely remarks that 'establishing definite similarities is hampered by the sketchiness of the New Testament accounts'.[30] To all this, we should add that the original post-resurrection appearances differed even more dramatically, inasmuch as, unlike the Christic visions, they conveyed for the first time the astonishing good news that God had vindicated the victimised Jesus and in doing so had initiated the coming general resurrection and the end of all things.

We have examined in detail three possible analogies to the Easter appearances: the experiences of grieving widows and widowers, mystical visions, and Christic visions.[31] Bereavement experiences, on close inspection, look far too dissimilar to be illuminating in any serious way. Mystical visions, while offering at least six points of comparison, on further scrutiny do not provide a close fit. Mystical visions of an imaginary kind, with which the New Testament authors also seem to be familiar, come across as somewhat different from what Paul and other Easter witnesses report of meetings with Jesus gloriously risen from the dead. Contemporary 'Christic' visions offer some similarity to what the New Testament says about the post-resurrection appearances of Jesus; these contemporary experiences have clearly made faith in his resurrection more credible for some, or even many, people. Nevertheless, they remain only somewhat similar. Judgments will differ on whether these visions illuminate in a striking fashion the nature of Jesus' post-resurrection appearances to which Peter, Paul, Mary Magdalene and other first Christians witnessed.

Beyond question, we may not claim instant credibility for these witnesses; we will come to this question in the next chapter. This chapter has had the preliminary task of showing how foundational beliefs and background theories can decisively shape assessments of what people have made of Jesus' fate after death, in general, and, in particular, of the nature of his post-mortem appearances to individuals and groups reported by the New Testament. Frequently analogies play their key part in shaping judgments for or against Easter faith. Whatever else we do, we need to probe and weigh these analogies. We need also to examine the other factors which may lend or deny credibility to faith in Jesus risen from the dead.

2
Historical Evidence and Its Limits

We believe about our own beliefs that they are
true – and hence not incompatible with whatever
will truly turn up.

Bas van Fraassen

I no longer believe in the resurrection. I have a
rational mind. I need a faith that respects reason.

Huxley Grieve

M UCH OF CHAPTER 1 ENGAGED IN a critical evaluation
of the views of others. We examined such background theories as the rejection of an all-powerful God, which rule out in
principle any belief in the resurrection of Christ. We also considered a range of analogies and their value for illuminating either
the resurrection itself or the Easter appearances. Right from the
opening criticisms of Luedemann and Marxsen, one issue was
already implicitly present through the chapter: what is the role
of historical knowledge for accepting or rejecting belief in Jesus
as risen from the dead? In the second century Celsus established
himself as the first in the line of those writers who have used
historical arguments to undermine the credibility of some central
events connected with Easter faith: for instance, the appearances
of the risen Christ to certain individuals and groups. Such
believers as Origen (ca. 185–ca. 254) were not convinced that
history undermined their faith; they have continued to respond

to Celsus and his successors by appealing (at least in part) to historical considerations to support it.

What then should be said about any connection between historical knowledge and resurrection faith? We can begin by setting aside two opposed answers: such faith is utterly independent of historical evidence; and such faith follows logically from historical evidence.

Two Extremes

In 1998, after reading an article which I had published on the resurrection of Christ, someone wrote to me and, among other things, asserted that 'the resurrection of Christ has nothing to do with the existence and history of human beings on our planet'. He added: 'It is a question of faith.' He spoke for all those who firmly separate reason and faith and consider thinking about history and trusting in God to belong to autonomous zones. They sometimes take their cue from what Immanuel Kant (1724–1804) wrote in the preface to the second edition of *The Critique of Pure Reason*: 'I must, therefore, put aside knowledge, to make room for belief.' Quite logically, my correspondent and those whom he represented remove the resurrection from the historical existence of human beings: they understand faith in the resurrection to belong to a 'storm-free zone' and to be quite untouched both by any investigations they might care to make into history and by any beliefs they hold about matters of history. As a matter of 'trust', my correspondent went on to say, the resurrection is not something which can 'be discovered and described by human beings'. Here we seem to glimpse part of the grounds for his position: only those realities which human beings can 'discover and describe' belong to history.

We will come back to this view of what belongs to history when reflecting on what the New Testament witnesses have to to say about the Easter appearances and the discovery of Christ's empty tomb. Here let me simply observe that, as with similar arguments about the commitment of faith having nothing to do with the exercise of human reason, my correspondent could not help using reason to support his claim that questions of faith and questions of reason are totally separate and autonomous. With all due respect to him, his position appears perilously close to being self-contradictory. He seems to use human reasoning to justify separating faith from reason.

One might also remark that, on any showing, 'the resurrection of Christ' must have something 'to do with the existence and history of human beings on our planet'. Unless Jesus had lived on our planet and died on a particular day in history, no one could have started talking about his resurrection from the dead. Any claims about his resurrection have, in that basic sense, something to do with the existence and history of human beings. Moreover, since all our languages belong to 'the existence and history' of human beings, the very fact that we speak about the resurrection of Christ brings it into the orbit of human existence and history.

Despite these obvious flaws in his argument, this correspondent serves, nevertheless, a useful purpose by alleging that the 'faith, trust, promise, and hope' which he finds in the resurrection have nothing to do with human history and historical reasoning.[1] He speaks for one extreme position. The other extreme is defended by such writers as Wolfhart Pannenberg (b. 1928) who argue that historical research can, more or less by itself, justify and engender faith. The Easter claim can be verified by rational argument.

Pannenberg has never wavered in his conviction that to accept the resurrection of Jesus is to make a judgment on the basis of historical evidence. Back in the 1960s he wrote: 'Whether or not a particular event happened two thousand years ago is not made certain by faith *but only by historical research*.'[2] He held that historians, although seen by many as threatening Christianity and its Easter faith, could and should pass a positive judgment on the evidence for Jesus' resurrection. In particular, the appearances of the risen Christ make the resurrection as reliably attested as any event in the ancient world. With his list of witnesses in 1 Corinthians 15:1–8, Paul intended to provide proof for the fact of Jesus' resurrection, 'a convincing historical proof by the standards of that time'.[3] Pannenberg also defended the discovery of the empty tomb as historically factual: it served to confirm the visions of the risen Lord. 'How could Jesus' disciples in Jerusalem,' he wrote, 'have proclaimed his resurrection if they could be constantly refuted merely by viewing the grave in which his body was interred?' The Easter message 'could not have been maintained in Jerusalem for a single day, for a single hour, if the emptiness of the tomb had not been established as a fact for all concerned'.[4]

Pannenberg went on to argue that the resurrection of Jesus made the end of all history present in advance and so disclosed the meaning of universal history. This universalising perspective did not, however, weaken Pannenberg's insistence on the specificity of the resurrection as a particular event. He described historical events as 'occurrences that actually happened at a definite time in the past'. Both 'the resurrection of Jesus' and 'the appearances of the resurrected Jesus' fulfil this description, for they 'really happened at a definite time in our world'. Pannenberg realised that there might be less difficulty about calling the Easter appearances historical. On those occasions the risen Christ 'made himself known in the midst of our reality at a very definite time, in a limited number of events, and to persons who are specifically named'. The *reality* of the resurrection itself, however, entails a new, transformed, post-mortem life which does not have a particular location in space and time and cannot be described directly but only through such analogies as 'rising from sleep' which we saw in Chapter 1. Yet, Pannenberg insisted, the resurrection-*event*, that transition from being an earthly reality to being a risen reality, occurred 'once at a definite time' and in a definite place (Jerusalem). Hence he would not tolerate a less than historical qualification for the resurrection. 'There is no justification,' he wrote, 'for affirming Jesus' resurrection as an event that really happened, if it is not to be affirmed as an historical event as such.' Since, he argued, the resurrection actually took place at a definite time in the past, it should be called historical and can be established by the research of historians.[5]

One immediately obvious objection to Pannenberg's case is that, if he is right, historians should be much more prominent among the ranks of those who accept the resurrection of Jesus. Through their profession they should be peculiarly competent to assess the evidence in favour of the Easter appearances and discovery of the empty tomb being actual events from the past. This should put historians into a privileged position to conclude that the resurrection of Jesus is an event that really happened. But, in fact, we do not find historians featuring disproportionately high on the list of believers. Pannenberg's response to this objection was anticipated by his requiring historians to approach the question of Jesus' resurrection with a truly open mind and not with the prior conviction that the dead cannot rise. Too many historians presumably share this bias and so rule out in advance the resurrection, betraying a one-sided orientation toward the typical at the expense of the historical, and a conviction that any resurrection is simply excluded by the rigid laws of nature. Pannenberg countered that modern science has broken with a deterministic world-view: the 'laws of nature' leave open the possibility of unfamiliar, even unique, events which are not determined by those laws. He argued that too many historians fail their profession because their background theories (about the impossibility of resurrection and other unique events) prevent them from investigating the claims about Jesus' resurrection.[6]

We will come back to other aspects of Pannenberg's case for the resurrection. But here I wish only to highlight his confidence that Jesus' rising from the dead can and should be verified by rational, historical argument. But moving beyond the two extreme positions (of my correspondent and Pannenberg), what do I hold about the link between historical knowledge and Christian faith in the risen Christ?

Historical Knowledge and Easter Faith

Not to raise the question of the part which historical knowledge plays in the genesis of Easter faith would be disturbingly at odds with professing Christianity to be an historical religion. This religion recognises certain, special events in history as the means *par excellence* by which God's revealing and saving self-communication has reached human beings. Moreover, Christian faith, as I maintain with many others, is a *reasonable* commitment, which, although it is not exclusively rational, points, nevertheless, to historical testimony when confessing what it believes about certain past events as special actions of God.

Christian faith, which is faith in the crucified *and risen* Jesus, cannot do without historical knowledge. Yet how much historical knowledge does it need? And who provides the 'ordinary' believer with the necessary knowledge? Rudolf Bultmann (1884–1976) and others answered these questions by drastically reducing the amount of historical knowledge needed for faith to the simple assertion 'that Jesus came', and decreeing that historians as such cannot be involved in the process by which even this minimum reaches the believer. 'Faith', he wrote, 'being personal decision, cannot be dependent upon an historian's labour.'[7] Bultmann had learned to isolate faith from history when he studied with Wilhelm Herrmann (1846–1922) at the University of Marburg. Herrmann summed up his position: 'It is a fatal error to attempt to establish the basis of faith by means of historical investigation. The basis of faith must be something fixed; the results of historical study are continually changing.'[8] Bultmann, Herrmann, and others back to the eighteenth century converge with my correspondent of 1998: the certainty of faith's decision cannot depend upon the uncertainties of historical knowledge. But does the experience of believers support this radical isolation of faith from history? Let me state and expound six theses, without engaging in a lengthy digression by developing them fully.

(1) **Faith in the crucified and risen Jesus cannot exist without some historical knowledge**. The amount of historical knowledge enjoyed by those who come to believe in the crucified and risen Jesus obviously varies a great deal. They may be notable writers and intellectuals like Malcolm Muggeridge (1903–90); he recorded his passage to such faith in several books on Jesus which examined what can be known historically from the Gospels and other sources (i.e. results derived from the 'labour' of historians). Other new

believers, such as those adults who receive baptism in the liturgy of Holy Saturday night, often pick up their knowledge of Jesus in less academic ways and not necessarily through reading works by professional historians and New Testament scholars. But in all cases the personal relationship of faith in Jesus Christ means being able to say something about his history, from birth to death and resurrection.

(2) **Such faith does not depend simply on historical knowledge**. While requiring the exercise of reason and not being merely a 'blind leap in the dark', faith depends and draws on things which go beyond reason and, specifically, go beyond historical reason. It is not mere historical evidence that justifies and supports one's faith. Without the grace of an interior divine illumination that accompanies the external presentation of the Christian message, no amount of historical knowledge, even the most extensive and sophisticated knowledge and even the best available biblical exegesis, will ever by itself bring about faith. Professional historians enjoy no such head-start over others in the race for faith. Their belief and our belief does not depend merely on how well it is supported by evidence.

In particular, faith entails a loving commitment and a trusting hope which freely goes beyond the limited evidence and enters into a personal relationship with Christ. 'Mere' knowledge, even the most critically acquired knowledge, so long as it remains bereft of graced illumination, love and hope, can never result in such faith. Faith in Christ may be compared with any life-long commitments to family and friends. Mere historical research into their previous activities and achievements could never provide the grounds for such commitments. In fact, most people would, I think, consider it insulting even to think of founding such loving commitments on the basis of background checks.

To sum up this second thesis: faith neither bases itself simply on historical knowledge nor forms a mere prolongation of such knowledge, as though the critical examination of history (e.g. evidence from biblical historians) could by itself establish and maintain faith. Christian faith does not exist independently of historical knowledge, but it cannot be reduced to it. 'Mere' historical evidence is not commensurate with the questions being asked and the issues at stake for faith.

It is intriguing that even Pannenberg, who insisted so much on faith being grounded upon historical evidence from the past, introduced other considerations when he elaborated the way in which the first disciples rightly understood what the resurrection of Jesus revealed. Since they already hoped for a general resurrection at the end of history, they were in a position to grasp something new: that the general resurrection and the end of all history had already been anticipated by Jesus' personal resurrection. Thus the truth of God was now revealed. But, even though solid historical evidence supports Pannenberg in crediting Jesus' disciples with such prior hopes for a general resurrection, how can people two thousand years later accept and share in those prior hopes and expect a future fulfilment for human beings in a general resurrection?[9] Pannenberg argued that such a hope for future resurrection proves its meaning and truth by being acted upon and standing 'the test today in the decisions of life'.[10] In other words, accepting now the expectations of the first disciples, which vitally shaped their full interpretation of Jesus' resurrection, comes through living with hope and (perhaps Pannenberg would add) love. A key element in his total picture of accepting the resurrection and the revelation it brought goes beyond historical truth to include trusting hope (and perhaps loving commitment).

(3) **The historical knowledge of believers is shaped by love and hope**. Elsewhere I have argued for the mutual interaction between knowing, loving, and the imagination of hope.[11] Love, for instance, facilitates knowledge, just as knowing makes it possible to love someone or something already known. This holds true also of historical knowledge. Believers know the historical truth and see meaning in the history of Jesus because they love him and find in him

the object of their deepest hopes, yet they commit themselves to him in love and trust after they have come to know
something of him and his history. Thus the historical knowledge of faith exemplifies two principles, not only '*nihil
volitum nisi precognitum* (nothing can be loved unless it is
already known)' but also '*nihil cognitum nisi prevolitum*
(nothing can be known unless it is already loved)'. St Augustine of Hippo (354–430) famously stressed the latter
principle, not least when he wrote about the interaction of
love and knowledge: '*Nemo nisi per amicitiam cognoscitur*' (*De
diversis questionibus*, 83. 71. 3). This could be paraphrased as
'you need to be a friend of someone before you truly know
him or her'. The eyes of love let us see reality and know the
truth.

(4) **Faith's historical knowledge belongs with its total
certainty**. For several centuries now, the firm claims of
faith about such matters as Jesus' death and resurrection have
faced routine censure. How can the certainty of faith tolerate
pervasive uncertainties in historical knowledge, or what
Herrmann called 'the continually changing' results of historical study? What this censure presupposes, among other
things, is that any assurance about matters of past history can
be detached from other characteristics of faith. However,
faith's firm answer to the question 'What can I know?'
belongs to the *one* act in which it also answers those other
two questions, 'What ought I to do?' and 'What may I hope
for?', and gives its allegiance to the person of Christ. A firm
confession of the historical truth about Jesus (summed up
in the Creed) belongs together in a lived unity with a full
commitment in trusting hope to his person.[12]

   Herrmann made an exaggerated claim when he declared
that 'the results of historical study are continually changing'.
The claim prompts the questions: All the results? Or only
some of them? Are they changing substantially or only in
secondary details and interpretations? Herrmann's version of
the results of historical research cries out for some heavy
qualifications.

One spots in Herrmann's 'denigration' of historical knowledge the long-term influence of Gotthold Ephraim Lessing (1729–81), whose minimalising approach to such knowledge took a two-pronged form: 'If no historical truth can be demonstrated, then nothing can be demonstrated by means of historical truths . . . Accidental truths of history can never become the proof of necessary truths of reason.'[13] Against this, one should argue that, although they cannot be 'demonstrated' by mathematical calculations, philosophical logic, or repeated scientific experiments, many historical truths can be established beyond any reasonable doubt. Mathematical calculations cannot demonstrate the existence and career of Alexander the Great in the fourth century BC. But converging historical evidence would make it absurd to deny that he lived and changed the political and cultural face of the Middle East. We cannot run the film backwards to regain contact with the past by literally reconstructing the assassination of Julius Caesar in 44 BC or the crucifixion of Jesus almost a hundred years later. Such historical events cannot be re-enacted in the way we can endlessly repeat scientific experiments in the laboratory. But only the lunatic fringe would cast doubt on these two violent deaths. *A priori* logic cannot demonstrate the existence of Augustine of Hippo (d. 430 AD). But to deny his existence and massive influence on subsequent European thought and society would be to exclude yourself from normal academic discussion about the history of Western ideas. The available data let us know a great deal that went on in the the ancient world, even if we cannot and should not try to 'demonstrate' our conclusions along the lines appropriate to mathematics, philosophy, and the natural sciences. There are very many historically certain truths from which we can argue and draw conclusions, including those which affect faith.

The main thrust of Lessing's case comes, however, in his second assertion: 'accidental truths of history can never become the proof of necessary truths of reason.' Even if we know with certainty many historical truths, they always remain contingent and accidental. These historical events, the truth of which we have established or – much more frequently – simply learned from others, neither had to happen at all nor had to happen precisely the way they did. In principle things could have gone differently in the lives of Alexander the Great, Augustine, Jesus, and Julius Caesar. Jesus might have been lynched and killed by stoning; he could have been crucified along with a dozen others; he might have appeared after his death to a group of one thousand and not to a group of five hundred (1 Corinthians 15:6). As such, historical truths neither enjoy the status of necessary, universal truths of reason, nor can they work to prove such truths of reason. But is that so tragic? In terms of this study of his resurrection, is it a fatal admission to grant that our knowledge of Jesus' death, burial, and post-mortem appearances does not rise 'above' the level of contingent truths? Strictly speaking, things could have gone differently.

Only someone like Lessing who was bewitched by the pursuit of necessary, universal truths of reason would deplore this historical situation. In the strict sense of the word, '*necessary* truths of reason' are tautologies, mathematical truths, and other *a priori* deductions which are in principle true always and everywhere and do not need the support of any empirical evidence. But how many people would base their lives on such truths? Historical experience and contingent truths have a power to shape and change human existence in a way never enjoyed by Lessing's timeless, universal truths of reason. In particular, 'accidental' truths from the story of Jesus and his most heroic followers have played a crucial role in the lives of millions of Christians. They have heard the reports of Jesus' life, death, and resurrection and the stories of his more saintly disciples, and found themselves awed, moved and changed. Both within Christianity and beyond, the concreteness of history repeatedly proves far more persuasive than any necessary truths of reason.

Furthermore, when historical claims are scrutinised, we

face a range of possibilities about our conclusions: from the utterly certain, through the highly probable, the solidly probable, the probable, and various shades of possibilities right down to the genuinely indeterminate. There is a range of historical conclusions which responsible scholars can firmly hold, even when they do not reach the status of utter certainty. They can make solidly probable cases and reach firm conclusions, without pretending to enjoy the complete certainty which would discount even the possibility that further evidence might come to light and disprove their conclusions.

Does this leave the assurance of faith – and its dependence on knowing events from the past – vulnerable, when historical knowledge may not be utterly certain about some important details (for instance, the emptiness of Jesus' tomb), and be open to the possibility of revision? And is it particularly shocking that Christians are 'at the mercy' of history, in much the same way as we all live at the mercy of reality itself, above all the human reality of other people, and yet continue to put our trust in them? In a large variety of ways we relate deeply to others and rely on their testimony. One of these ways concerns the history of salvation and, in particular, the life, death, and resurrection of Jesus. When I trust that new evidence from research scholars will not shatter the picture which I cherish of the historical Jesus' life, death, and resurrection, I am no more indulging reckless confidence than when I trust that I have not been, for instance, horribly mistaken in family matters by presuming that 'this man' is 'my father'. Life would be intolerable if we decided to live under the persistent fear of being confronted with the startling news that reality is not what we have taken it to be and we have been proved horribly wrong. We admit that it may be logically possible that we have been deluded, but we are confident that it is not so. It is possible that my mother had a secret lover and I have been mistaken for decades over my paternity. But I am confident that this is not so, and would never dream of digging up my father's remains to exclude any possible doubt by having a DNA test performed. Such 'definitive' evidence would betray and not enhance my parents' memory.

To spend my life morbidly preoccupied with the possibility that someone else fathered me would destroy my relationship with my parents. Similarly, nothing could be more destructive of my relationship with my spouse than constantly and anxiously anticipating the possibility of emotional rejection and unfaithfulness by asking myself, 'What will I do if she gets tired of me and has an affair with someone else?' The case of faith in the crucified and risen Christ seems similar. To focus persistently on the possibility that new historical evidence could turn up and refute our belief in Jesus would exclude any workable and worthwhile faith. In other words, the 'risk' of faith is not unlike our basic human belief in the identity of our parents and in the fidelity of our spouse, friends and relatives, inasmuch as such belief involves historical claims which are vulnerable in principle.

Here we might make the analogy more precise by distinguishing our relationship to (a) parents and siblings from (b) our relationship to spouse and friends. Both (a) and (b) are vulnerable in principle, but in different ways. In the case of (a), we grow up within a given situation rather than a relationship we have personally chosen; our commitment to parents and siblings comes from our being born into a particular family. This case resembles that of 'cradle Christians', who grow up with a commitment to Easter faith and a relationship to Christ. In their adult years they can reflect on this faith relationship and allow it to deepen or else can let it slip and even reject it outright. But in their earlier years this faith relationship has been a 'given' of their existence. In the case of (b), we choose our spouses and friends. Along with spontaneous feelings and desires, such reasonable grounds as shared interests, common values and similar expectations usually play their part in our making such commitments. We come to these commitments, rather than being born and raised with them, just as non-believers can come to faith and a commitment to Christ. They do so usually because they have *also* found the evidence (both historical and otherwise) and motives for such faith to be reasonable and convincing. In short, the analogy proposed can be refined to cover those who start life as 'insiders' to faith and those who start as 'outsiders' and may become 'insiders'.

What I am arguing for here is the view that the confession of faith involves an historical risk when we accept the testimony of others – in this case, testimony about the crucified and risen Christ. But we need to add at once two riders. Faith does not depend simply upon historical knowledge (thesis two) And the historical risk is part of the general risk of reality as the believer understands and accepts reality.

(5) **Vulnerability affects the knowing, loving and hoping of faith.** It is a fact of experience that Christian believers can waver and cease to confess that Jesus lived, died and rose to bring salvation to the world. They may do so because they judge that historical research has disproved the resurrection of Jesus. Or they may make no secret of the fact that they now feel unable to maintain either the loving commitment of faith or a hopeful attitude towards the future. Such failure in commitment or confidence will tamper with faith's confession of past events, and vice versa. Things which hold men and women back from full love and total trust can sap the firmness of their faith, as much as doubts about the truth of the historical confession at the heart of the Christian Creed. In short, faith is neither totally made (thesis two) or totally unmade (this thesis) by the answer to the question: What can we know historically about the past events of salvation history? The knowing, loving and hoping of faith are intertwined, and faith remains humanly vulnerable at each level.

(6) **Faith's knowing, loving and hoping involve the universal and the particular.** From the start of Christianity, when believers confessed that 'Jesus is Lord', they did so because they believed that 'God had raised him from the

dead' (e.g. Romans 10:9). Their faith involved holding that through his particular, historical existence, death and resurrection Jesus enjoyed a universal function as *the* Revealer and Saviour. Thus their confession could be summed up by saying that 'Jesus (the particular person from Nazareth) is the Christ (the Lord of the universe).' Their questions about what any and every human being could know, do and hope for found a precise answer in the particular person of Jesus.

On the one hand, by being rooted in history, faith avoids any flight to a set of vague generalities. On the other hand, by recalling the need to face universal issues, faith resists the temptation to reduce Christianity to some kind of mere nostalgic interest in the history of Jesus. In brief, faith finds salvation in both the historical (Jesus) and the universal (Christ).

Historical Evidence

My six theses have been largely concerned with broader issues about faith and history. What of the specific case of belief in Jesus as risen from the dead? What degree of probability does this belief enjoy from the historical evidence? What evidential input can we cite in support of resurrection faith? Arguments take the form of the most plausible explanation to account for the data at hand. They may do this by offering a 'global' explanation or by concentrating on such particulars as reports of the appearances of the risen Christ. Global explanations regularly follow a movement from demonstrable effects to their only adequate cause, the resurrection of Jesus. Let us see several examples, which can be classified under two forms: arguments from the spread of Christianity and from the novelties to be explained.

The Spread of Christianity

After a short public career, which at the most lasted three or four years, Jesus was abandoned by nearly all his close followers, crucified as a messianic pretender, and apparently rejected by the God (Mark 15:34) whom he had confidently proclaimed as 'Abba' or 'Father dear'. Yet within a few years the reform

[39]

movement which he had proclaimed within Judaism spread explosively to become a world religion. How can one account most plausibly for this phenomenon?

Some point to certain historical reasons which helped the spread of Christianity: for instance, the existence of the *pax romana*, which supported relatively easy communication in the first-century Mediterranean world. Add too that slaves, women, and many of the working classes found no other religious option more attractive than Christianity. Nevertheless, what do matters look like if we compare Jesus with other religious founders? A number of 'this-worldly' factors, which help explain the propagation of Buddhism, Confucianism, and Islam by the Gautama (ca. 563–ca. 483 BC), Confucius (ca. 550–478 BC) and Muhammed (ca. 570–632 AD), respectively, do not apply to Christianity. In the case of these three founders, time was on their side. Gautama passed most of his long life teaching the way of enlightenment. The Chinese sage Confucius also spent years spreading his wisdom and attracting disciples, until he died and was buried with great pomp outside Kufow. A wealthy wife and then military victories helped Muhammed to gather followers and propagate his teaching. As the recognised prophet of Arabia, he died in Medina and was buried there. In these three instances we can point to publicly verifiable causes which furthered the spread, respectively, of Buddhism, Confucianism and Islam: the long careers of the founders, financial resources, and success in battle. In the case of Christianity, the founder enjoyed none of these advantages: his public career was extremely short, he lacked military and financial support, and his life ended in humiliating failure and a disgraceful death on a cross. After all this, the subsequent propagation of the message of universal salvation in his name remains an enigmatic puzzle unless we admit a cause (the resurrection) adequate to account for the effect.[14]

Novelties to Explain

Certain authors, as we saw in Chapter 1, try to account for claims about Jesus' resurrection as resulting naturally from the psychological state and religious convictions of his disciples. Is this explanation historically plausible? Some of Jesus' disciples came to accept him as the messianic agent of divine salvation (e.g. Mark 8:29; 11:1–10). But it is doubtful that they understood and accepted anything which he said about himself as the suffering Son of Man (e.g. Mark 8:31). Then he was executed on the charge of being a messianic pretender and even a blasphemer. What options were available for his disciples after the crucifixion? Could they have modified their messianic belief in him and proposed him to be another martyred prophet like John the Baptist and others before him? Hardly, it seems to me. To be crucified was not only to suffer an utterly cruel and humiliating form of execution, but also to die under a religious curse (Galatians 3:13) and 'outside the camp' of God's covenanted people (Hebrews 13:12–13). In other words, crucifixion was seen as the death of a criminal and godless man who perished away from God's presence and in the place and company of irreligious men. To honour anyone who was put to death in such a way was an awful and profound scandal (1 Corinthians 1:23). Given that crucifixion was such a disgrace, could Jesus' disciples have proclaimed him *even as a martyred prophet*?

In fact, they began preaching the crucified Jesus as the divinely endorsed Messiah risen from the dead to bring salvation for all. The notion of a Messiah who failed, suffered, was crucified and then rose from the grave was simply foreign to pre-Christian Judaism. Since their previous religious beliefs could not have led Jesus' disciples to make such startlingly new claims about him, what triggered off this religious novelty? Where did it come from, if not from the resurrection of Jesus himself?

Some scholars, when elaborating the effect-cause argument, have stressed the centrality of the theme of resurrection in early Christian preaching. Over thirty years ago C. F. Evans showed how 'the central place of the resurrection faith in the New Testament' could not be explained or expected 'either from contemporary Judaism or from the preaching' of Jesus.[15] A theme which had hitherto been at best on the religious periphery moved to centre stage. Neither the Jewish background nor the teaching of Jesus himself sufficiently accounts for the given effect: the central importance which the New Testament attributes to the resurrection. Unless Jesus was raised from the dead, we have no cause adequate to explain the centrality of the resurrection in the faith, preaching and theology of the first Christians. In a lecture delivered in 2002, N. T. Wright developed a similar argument. An examination of first-century Judaism and the surrounding world shows a variety of beliefs about the existence (or non-existence) of life after death. But we find nothing which closely resembles what the first Christians began proclaiming about Jesus and the nature of his resurrection. Since that preaching could hardly have come from prior beliefs, the historian must look for another explanation: the event of Jesus' resurrection itself.[16]

A specific form of this effect-cause argument has been mounted by Pannenberg and others about an observable shift in religious expectations. In late Judaism some cherished a hope that the resurrection of all the dead and a general judgment would terminate human history. Then the followers of Jesus began announcing that this one individual had already been raised to a glorious existence which anticipated the end of all history. What caused such a new element in religious history – the shift from an expectation of general resurrection at the end of history to the proclamation of something that no one had expected, the glorious, final resurrection of one individual which has already initiated that end? What prompted this radical change in expectations held by a significant group of first-century Jews about the fulfilment of human life through resurrection? Historians of late Judaism have documented the effect, a remarkable change in expectations. A plausible cause is available: the actual resurrection of Jesus from the dead.[17]

Once again, just as with arguments about the founding and spread of Christianity, we cannot characterise Pannenberg's argument as a strictly cogent proof. An alternate scenario might be imagined. Some first-century Jews who shared a hope for a general resurrection to come at the end of history could have reflected on the traditions about such individuals as Enoch (Genesis 5:24) and Elijah (2 Kings 2:9–12) being caught up to heaven and escaping death. This might have triggered a development about one or more special individuals being raised from the dead even before the general resurrection took place. Such a scenario does not, however, strike me as truly plausible. The role ascribed to the risen Jesus for the salvation of the whole world differs remarkably from any beliefs about Enoch and Elijah.[18]

Where Evans, Wright, Pannenberg and others have fashioned effect-cause arguments out of demonstrable changes in the beliefs of Jesus' first disciples after his death and burial, Richard Swinburne[19] has named the new celebration of Sunday as the effect to be accounted for. Why did these Jewish disciples no longer give priority to Saturday and turn 'the first day of the week' into *the* day for meeting and worshipping together? What made them hold this day so special that they not only changed their day but also their manner of worship (1 Corinthians 11:23–26)? An obvious reason is close at hand: Sunday was the day when his tomb was discovered to be open and empty, and the day when they first encountered the risen Jesus.

Without being a strict proof, this argument enjoys a certain plausibility. Those who reject it need to produce an alternate explanation as to why the disciples of Jesus changed their special day of worship from the Jewish Sabbath to the Christian Sunday?

Appearances and Empty Tomb

Any apologetic for the factuality of Jesus' resurrection from the dead must be specific in establishing that the accounts of the Easter appearances and of the discovery of the open and empty tomb are historically reliable. Unlike the second-century apocryphal Gospel of Peter (9.35–11.35), neither St Paul nor the Gospel writers allege that anyone witnessed the actual event of Jesus' resurrection. The New Testament repeatedly names the appearances and the discovery of the empty tomb as the two dramatic causes which let the disciples know that Jesus had risen from the dead. Some of them saw him gloriously alive, and all of them could verify what some female disciples had discovered, his open and empty tomb.

The early Christian proclamation (e.g. 1 Corinthians 15:5–7; Luke 24:34), Paul (1 Corinthians 9:1; 15:8; Galatians 1:12, 16), the four Gospels (Matthew 28; Luke 24; John 20 and 21; and, by implication, Mark 16:7), Acts (e.g. 1:3; 10:40–41; 13:31) and the appendix to Mark (16:9–20) attest that the risen Jesus appeared both to various individuals and to groups of witnesses, above all 'the twelve' or 'the eleven', as Luke 24:33 more accurately calls them after the defection of Judas. These appearances of the living Jesus were the primary way the disciples came to know that he was risen from the dead.

But how credible are these reports of the risen Jesus' appearances? Why believe that Mary Magdalene, Peter, Paul and other New Testament witnesses genuinely saw Jesus risen from the dead? The sources diverge on secondary matters. Who was the first to see the risen Lord? Mary Magdalene (John 20:14–18, Matthew 28:9–10) or Peter (1 Corinthians 15:5; Luke 24:34)? Where did the appearances take place – in Galilee (Mark 16:7) or in and around Jerusalem (Luke 24)? Yet the Easter proclamation, Paul and the evangelists agree on the primary fact of appearances to certain individuals and to groups – in particular, 'the Twelve' (1 Corinthians 15:5).

At the same time, they show little interest in describing and explaining the nature of the appearances. My 1998 correspondent was off target when he implied that those who disagree with him propose a resurrection which can 'be discovered and described by human beings'. Our New Testament sources never suggest that someone could set out to 'discover' and 'describe' either the risen Jesus or the event of his resurrection. They report that certain witnesses were confronted with him risen from the dead and with his open and empty tomb. To allege that the resurrection of Jesus was (or is) something human beings purport to 'discover and describe' and then criticise this attempt is to train guns on a purely imaginary target.

Some try to reduce the impact of the witness to the risen Jesus' appearances by linking them to a range of supposedly similar phenomena, as we have seen in Chapter 1. But a gap remains between the Easter experiences and those phenomena (e.g. the psychodynamics of grief and guilt to which Gerd Luedemann appeals). Luedemann, like others before him, also writes off the appearances as ecstatic group hallucinations.[20] Such a counter-explanation would be more feasible if the New Testament had reported only one appearance and that to a particular group on a particular day. Instead, it reports appearances over a period of time and to different groups and different individuals. The major 'ecstatic' group experience came with the account of Pentecost (Acts 2:1–4). But that episode involved receiving the Holy Spirit and not seeing the risen Christ.

Theories of hallucination frequently suppose that after the death and burial of Jesus the disciples were eagerly expecting him to rise from the dead, and so deceived themselves into thinking that they saw him. The evidence from the New Testament suggests, however, that they did not persuade themselves, but needed to be persuaded when the risen Christ showed himself to them (e.g. Matthew 28:16–18; Luke 24:36–43). Moreover, Paul remains the classical difficulty for those who espouse any such hallucination hypothesis. Far from hoping to meet the risen Christ, he persecuted the early Christians. Paul's encounter with the risen Christ occurred at a later time and in a different place from the other Easter appearances (see 1 Corinthians 15:8; Galatians 1:11–24). Any hypothesis of an 'enthusiastic' chain reaction in which the disciples one after another hallucinated an 'appearance' of the risen Jesus cannot cover the case of Paul. From the time of Celsus in the second century,[21] the hallucination hypothesis has been tried and found wanting.

Admittedly the witnesses to the appearances of the risen Christ are a relatively small number. But it would make little or no difference if there were thousands of such witnesses. Stubborn sceptics, like David Hume and William Clifford (of whom more in the next chapter), would still argue that it is never rational to believe such witnesses. The fact that the witnesses provided by the New Testament are not very numerous does not seem particularly relevant.

As regards the discovery of the empty tomb, authors of the New Testament show themselves aware that the empty tomb did not by itself prove the resurrection of Jesus. In John's Gospel, for instance, Mary Magdalene, on discovering the tomb to be open and empty, thinks that someone or other has shifted the body to another place: 'They have taken the Lord out of the tomb, and we do not know where they have laid him' (John 20:2). Furthermore, the evangelists do not agree about secondary details, which concern principally the women and the angel(s). The four Gospels offer differing answers to such questions as: How many women went to the tomb? Why did they go there? How many angels intervened? Where were they? What did they do and say? What emotions did the women show in the face of the angelic presence and message? What did the women do afterwards? Yet the four evangelists, Mark (followed by Matthew and Luke) and John (with his different tradition), agree on the primary datum. To her astonishment, at least one woman (Mary Magdalene) found Jesus' tomb to be open and empty two days after his death and burial. But is this claim historically reliable? The role of women in Mark 15:42–47 and 16:1–8 suggests that the first Christians, at least those in Jerusalem, knew about Jesus' burial and the location of his tomb. But was his tomb discovered to be open and empty shortly after his death?

One argument against the historicity of the empty tomb which merits the most attention is the view which takes the tomb stories to be merely legendary elaborations or illustrations of the message of the resurrection.[22] Put more precisely, this argument holds that Mark 16:1–8 and the subsequent empty tomb stories neither convey nor intend to convey any factual information about the state of Jesus' tomb, since they were simply imaginative ways of announcing the resurrection and entirely derivative from the central proclamation of the resurrection of the crucified Jesus and his subsequent appearances (1 Corinthians 15:3–8). The elaboration is often supposed to have taken place over the ten or fifteen years between the report of the appearances offered by 1 Corinthians 15 and the writing of Mark's Gospel. Sometimes, as we shall see below and in Chapter 4, Mark himself is alleged to have created the empty tomb story to illustrate the fundamental traditions of the resurrection and the appearances.

The hypothesis that the traditions of the risen Jesus' appearances led to the imaginative creation of an empty tomb story is flimsy. Careful exegesis indicates that the two traditions (of the appearances and the empty tomb) have independent origins. The differences are such that it is hard to see the first producing the second.

Major elements found in 1 Corinthians 15:3–8 simply do not turn up in Mark 16:1–8: the appeal to the scriptures (1 Corinthians 15:3, 4), the atoning death 'for our sins' (1 Corinthians 15:3), the title 'Christ' (1 Corinthians 15:3) which seems to have already become a second name for Jesus, and the appearances to 'more than five hundred brethren', to James, to 'all the apostles', and to Paul (1 Corinthians 15:6–8). Mark's empty tomb story promises appearances only to the 'disciples' and Peter (Mark 16:7). Mark's narrative contains some major items of which 1 Corinthians 15:3–8 knows nothing at all: the discovery of the empty tomb by three (named) women, the interpreting angel, and the promise of appearances *in Galilee*. (Paul's list provides no locale for any of the appearances.) Even a cursory comparison between 1 Corinthians 15:3–8 and Mark 16:1–8 illustrates the dubiousness of the thesis that the message of the resurrection and the appearances led to the formation of empty tomb stories. These stories seem to be derived from independent origins. But are the empty tomb accounts essentially reliable?

Apologists for the empty tomb stories being basically reliable normally produce a variety of arguments: for instance, the central place of the women in these stories. In the oldest version (Mark 16:1–8) three women were astonished to find Jesus' tomb to be open and empty on the first Easter Sunday morning. If this story were simply a legend created by one or more early Christians, they would presumably have attributed the discovery of the empty tomb to male disciples rather than to women. In first-century Palestine women and slaves were, for all intents and purposes, disqualified as valid witnesses.[23] The natural thing for someone making up a legend about the empty tomb would have been to have ascribed the discovery to men and not to women. Legend-makers do not normally invent positively unhelpful material.

Critics have attempted to rebut this argument in various ways.

First, it was known that by the first Easter Sunday the male disciples had already fled from Jerusalem and not yet returned to the city. Hence Mark or whoever made up the story of the discovery of the empty tomb had no choice; the protagonists had to be female disciples, as these were known to have stayed behind in Jerusalem.[24] This leaves us with a curiously mixed picture about the 'moral constraints' felt by Mark or whoever made up the empty tomb story. On the one hand, he respected a precise and reliable piece of information which the existing tradition recalled about the whereabouts of some followers of Jesus on a given day: only female disciples were in the city on the first Easter Sunday morning. But, on the other hand, he felt free to invent from nothing the narrative about their visit to Jesus' tomb and the discovery they made. One wonders how such a story would have struck its first readers. They knew that female disciples were around on that morning but had hitherto known nothing whatsoever of the women visiting the tomb and discovering it to be open and empty.

Other critics dismiss the significance of the point about women being invalid witnesses. Yes, they argue, that point would tell in favour of the historical reliability of the empty tomb story *if it had originated early and in Palestine*. But, they claim, it had a later, Hellenistic origin. Hence those who created the empty tomb story and their first readers would not find the witness of women necessarily embarrassing or counter-productive. Obviously one key feature of this debate bears on the dating for the final composition of Mark's Gospel: many scholars suggest around 70 AD or even earlier. A second important question concerns the Hellenistic or Greco-Roman elements detectable in what Mark wrote. Could this first-century Christian, deeply committed to the new faith, most probably of Jewish background, obviously steeped in the Jewish Scriptures, and of no great literary talent have drawn on Greco-Roman ideas (e.g. about someone's translation to a heavenly existence) in using or composing a 'fiction' as a way of proclaiming Jesus' resurrection from the dead? Mark 1—15 shows this evangelist setting the story of Jesus in the context of Jewish salvation history; these chapters are permeated with quotations

and echoes of the Jewish scriptures, as Mark goes about illustrating how Jesus fulfilled various Jewish (and not Greco-Roman)
motifs. Can Greco-Roman thought-forms be invoked to prove
the master-key to what Mark wrote in his final eight verses? One
notable supporter of this thesis, Adela Yarbro Collins, has to
admit that 'it is hard to find' in Mark much influence from Greco-
Roman literature.[25] If so, it hardly seems convincing to claim that
he changed character and unexpectedly used Hellenistic sources
for his final chapter.

These paragraphs have been sketching some of the questions
which are relevant for those who wish to assess the historical
reliability of the traditions about the appearances of the risen
Jesus and his empty tomb. In earlier publications I have dedicated
many more pages to these particular issues.[26] Yet how much does
such historical argument contribute to the making of Easter faith?

The Limits of Evidence

Beyond question, scrutinising the historical evidence which supports belief in Christ's resurrection has its value. This exercise
can feed into a cumulative case for such belief and, negatively
speaking, can also show up the weaknesses in various counter-
explanations about what happened – or did not happen – in the
aftermath of the crucifixion and burial of Jesus. But limiting ourselves to a scrutiny of the evidence might unwittingly cater to
some silent expectation that belief in the resurrection is over-
whelmingly rational. Why, despite thesis two above, should we
expect belief in the resurrection and, for that matter, belief in
God, which is closely connected with Easter faith, to be an over-
whelmingly rational matter? Rational argument, while relevant to
religious belief, is not a sufficient condition for acquiring it, or –
more accurately – receiving it. Experience constantly shows how
the mere force of argument is never enough by itself to convert
someone to Christian faith. If the (historical) evidence were
sufficient to establish or conclusively confirm resurrection belief,
such belief should be utterly convincing to all those willing to
weigh the evidence and draw the obvious conclusions from it.
Yet this would be a return to Pannenberg's position (outlined

above) and to its obvious rebuttal. If Pannenberg is correct, those best able to evaluate the evidence (i.e. historians) should be much more prominent among the ranks of those who agree with the conclusion that Jesus was raised from the dead. Moreover, by unilaterally attending to the evidence, we risk identifying *knowing* the resurrection with *the evidence for it*.

But here, as elsewhere in life, we know more than the evidence. In close personal relationships, for instance, the evidence at our disposal is not all that we know. Knowing those whom we love is much more than simply knowing a certain number of facts about them, 'facts' which the available evidence might establish. 'Knowing' people goes well beyond merely 'knowing of' them or 'knowing about' them; knowing them can be expressed as experiencing them directly, deeply and enduringly.

All of this suggests that the issue of Easter should be better expressed in terms of knowing the risen Jesus and in terms of the conditions for the possibility of experiencing him deeply and enduringly. My next chapter takes up this knowing and its conditions.

3
Testimony and Experience

No one can say 'Jesus is Lord' except by the
Holy Spirit.

St Paul, 1 Corinthians 12:3

Holy things for the holy people. One is holy, one
is Lord, Jesus Christ. O, taste and see that the
Lord is good.

St Cyril of Jerusalem, *Mystagogical Catecheses*, 5.19–20

Each separate argument would not suffice of
itself for showing perfectly Christ's resurrection,
yet all taken together establish it completely.

St Thomas Aquinas, *Summa Theologiae*, 3a. 55.6 ad 2.

EVERY NOW AND THEN we hear of some celebrity being
named as the father of a child born out of wedlock and,
despite his initial disclaimers, being proved to be such by a DNA
test. This evidence clearly establishes his paternity, but – far from
furthering life-giving interpersonal relationships – it signals their
breakdown. On the basis of such evidence,[1] people do not 'know'
or experience each other in a deeply enriching way.

William Kingdon Clifford (1845–79) was a classical supporter
of the case for staying within the limits of evidence alone. A
fellow of Trinity College, Cambridge, he was appointed professor
of mathematics at University College, London in 1871 and
elected a fellow of the Royal Society in 1874. He died of

consumption at only 33 years of age in 1879. In his 'Ethics of Belief' Clifford passed over the personal dimension of knowledge and belief when he proposed a famous (or should one say notorious?) axiom: 'It is wrong always, everywhere, and for anyone to believe anything on insufficient evidence.'[2] In 'The Will to Believe', a paper first published in 1896, William James (1842–1810), a professor of Harvard University, commented on Clifford's axiom:

> Believe nothing, he tells us, keep your mind in suspense forever, rather than by closing it on insufficient evidence incur the awful risk of believing lies . . . he who says, 'Better go without belief for ever than believe a lie!' merely shows his own preponderant private horror of becoming a dupe. He may be critical of many of his desires and fears, but this fear he slavishly obeys. He cannot imagine anyone questioning its binding force. For my own part, I have also a horror of being duped; but I can believe that worse things than being duped may happen to a man in this world: so Clifford's exhortation has to my ears a thoroughly fantastic sound. It is like a general informing his soldiers that it is better to keep out of battle for ever than risk a single wound. Not so are victories either over enemies or over nature gained. Our errors are surely not such awfully solemn things. In a world where we are so certain to incur them in spite of all our caution, a certain lightness of heart seems healthier than this excessive nervousness on their behalf.[3]

Clifford's axiom, we should add, makes light of the fact that our most significant beliefs are caused in us by, or are directed towards, persons. Primarily we believe in someone, not in something, as when we believe in someone sufficiently to enter matrimony with that person, or when – right from infancy – we accept countless beliefs on the authority of our parents and teachers.

Clifford recognised that there is a 'vast body of knowledge which is daily growing upon the world', and he had to acknowledge that 'neither we nor any other one person can possibly test a hundredth part of it by immediate experience or observation' (p. 207). Yet he insisted on 'the universal duty of questioning all that we believe' (p. 205). One wonders how such universal questioning could be practised and how it could be reconciled with Clifford's admission: 'we may believe the statement of another person, when there is reasonable ground for supposing that he knows the matter of which he speaks and that he is speaking the truth so far as he knows it' (p. 220). But what could count as 'sufficient evidence' to establish reasonable grounds for making these two suppositions?

Clifford's axiom looks very much like a personal 'intuition' or even an unsupported assertion rather than the conclusion of a 'scientific' argument. What could count as 'sufficient evidence' to establish that 'it is wrong always, everywhere, and for anyone to believe anything on insufficient evidence'? How could Clifford have convincingly established the truth of his axiom? One might turn his axiom on its head and come up with something that *prima facie* might sound a little more convincing: 'It is wrong always, everywhere, and for anyone to disbelieve anything on insufficient evidence.' Even so, how could one go about establishing the truth of this alternate axiom?

In 'The Ethics of Belief' Clifford himself did not always display an intellectual integrity consistent with his axiom by questioning all that he believed and disbelieved. He summarily dismissed pilgrimages to Lourdes as catering to 'immoral and debasing superstition' (p. 214), sneered at Australian aborigines for continuing to tie the head of their hatchets to the side of the handle (p. 215), and expressed equal contempt for Spanish naval engineers coping with iron steamships and 'savages' trying to wind up watches (p. 216). Did Clifford have 'sufficient' evidence to justify these harsh judgments? When criticising Clifford's views, William James drily commented: it is not 'pure reason' that 'settles our opinions' (p. 225). Even if he did not cite Clifford's contempt for the shrine of Lourdes, the words of James apply with precision. Without 'even looking at the evidence' for cures, Clifford found 'no use' for Catholic 'feelings' about such pilgrimages being valuable for both the sick and healthy. Hence he disbelieved 'all facts and theories' connected with Lourdes (p. 226). James reached the heart of the matter in his conclusion: 'When the Cliffords [of this world] tell us how sinful it is to be Christians on such "insufficient evidence", insufficiency is really the last thing they have in mind. For them the evidence is absolutely sufficient' – but for the opposite position. 'They believe so completely in an anti-Christian order of the universe that there is no living option. Christianity is a dead hypothesis from the start' (p. 228).

In 'The Ethics of Belief' Clifford never explicitly raised the question of the resurrection. But presumably he would have held that 'it is wrong, always, everywhere, and for anyone to believe in the resurrection on insufficient evidence'. Yet could there ever be 'sufficient evidence' for this belief? To borrow a remark which the French pope in Maurice West's *The Clowns of God* makes to his sceptical German friend, 'Karl, old friend, there is never enough evidence.' A more solemn answer to a Clifford-style call to provide sufficient evidence for Easter faith would be provided by discussing in detail an earlier challenge to the resurrection – that which came from David Hume (1711–76). For Hume there could never be enough evidence to justify believing in the resurrection; in his view, it is never rational to believe that a resurrection from the dead had happened. Not even countless witnesses could ever justify any reasonable person accepting the resurrection of Christ.[4]

In responding to Clifford and Hume, we might follow others in examining the 'uniformity of nature' and the possibility of exceptions. It is even more fundamental to question whether 'remaining within the limits of evidence alone' – as Clifford and Hume understand 'evidence' – is the path to knowing in faith the risen Christ (or to rejecting such a knowing in faith) and to knowing what is closely related this issue, belief in God. It takes personal testimony and personal experience to bring about the conditions for such 'knowing' (or for rejecting it).

Testimony to the Risen Christ

Testimony provides a central way in which we acquire and develop our knowledge.[5] In the long years of our education we have to take many things on the authority of our parents and our teachers. When our formal education ends, we continue to accept many things on the word of accredited experts in such fields as medicine, biology, and other sciences. Provided we too have the competence and could repeat, for example, some scientific experiments, we might check for ourselves some of the beliefs which we first accepted from the testimony of experts. But, however wide-ranging our personal expertise, we could never conceivably verify everything which we are told by medical scientists, cosmologists and other experts. We simply do not have the time to do this. Whether we like it or not, over wide ranges of human knowledge we have to rely on the testimony of reliable witnesses.

When we turn to the way in which the word of witnesses functions in such areas as family life, courts of law and the transmission of the Christian message, we move into the area of historical testimony. In these cases we cannot make time run backwards and directly experience for ourselves events to which the witnesses testify. The popularity of science fiction books and films which involve time machines suggests that many people would like to go back in time and experience for themselves some events which deeply interest them. But they cannot do so. In historical matters, along with such pointers as archaeological and forensic evidence, we have to rely on the oral and, especially, the written word of witnesses. Believing witnesses in courts of law, family life and the transmission of the Christian message can impinge deeply on our lives and the lives of others, and even shape them for ever. But why should we believe the witnesses? What is involved in accepting their testimony to what they have personally experienced?

In the case of the original, apostolic witnesses to the resurrection of Jesus and the long chain of dependent witnesses who have passed on to us the original testimony, much more is involved than merely believing seemingly reliable witnesses who testify to events in which they were personally present and involved. Firstly, it means believing the testimony of persons who encountered the risen Jesus in a special kind of experience which, at least partly (see Chapter 1 above), was peculiar to them. Even if we had been alive in the early first century, we could not have repeated their experience of the risen Jesus and so have verified it for ourselves. We might have checked the empty tomb of Jesus for ourselves by repeating the visit of the holy women. But, *pace* the case of Thomas the Twin (John 20:24–29), we could not have personally verified in that way the testimony to the appearances by somehow prevailing on the risen Lord to appear also to us. Here we find ourselves in a position analogous to that of the Corinthian and Galatian Christians. When writing letters in which he cited his own encounter with the risen Jesus (1 Corinthians 9:1; 15:8; Galatians 1:12, 16), Paul rebuked them for various failures in belief and behaviour. But he never reproached them for not having seen the Lord, as he personally had in a special encounter which initiated his apostolic ministry. Paul never wrote: 'What kind of Christians are you? Why hasn't the Lord appeared also to you?' Accepting the testimony of the Easter witnesses involves accepting their word about an experience which was, at least partly, peculiar to them and non-repeatable. Secondly, it means answering fundamental questions about the nature, meaning and destiny of our own existence and that of the whole cosmos. It entails letting the way we construe reality be transformed, and calls for new ways of being and acting in the Church and the world. This needs to be explained further.

The apostolic witnesses to the post-resurrection appearances testified not only to the appearances but also to what those appearances triggered off: changed ways of living and a new set of hopes. In 1 Corinthians and Galatians, Paul spells out at length his transformed ways of living, as well as his new hopes for sharing in a glorious resurrection through Christ (1 Corinthians 15:12–58). In his subsequent Letter to the Romans the Apostle sketched his expectations that the whole created universe would also share in the glory that is to come (Romans 8:18–25).

Thus those who testified to the resurrection proclaim a

message which included but goes beyond the post-resurrection appearances. This full Easter message began with the apostolic witnesses and was then passed on in very many places, by innumerable believers, and over a very long period of time. By accepting this Easter testimony, we put our trust in the persons who witness to this message. They 're-present' to us the full event of the resurrection; without their witness, the event would be lost to us. The veracity of their Easter testimony becomes credible to the extent that it has led them to a deeper union with God and with one another. Lives of holiness and loving service to others make their witness believable. The presence of the risen Christ 'comes through' the way they have lived out and continue to live out their Easter faith.

What happens here also holds true, in various ways and degrees, when we trustingly and even lovingly accept personal testimony to events which otherwise would never be known to us and would never affect us. In courts of law, when jurors find certain witnesses credible, they feel 'in tune' with them. Even more so, when parents tell their children the story of their courtship and marriage, out of love sons and daughters spontaneously believe such stories. If children feared being credulous and, in the spirit of W. K. Clifford, demanded 'sufficient evidence' before accepting their parents' testimony, this would reveal and reinforce some kind of breakdown in family relations and in mutual trust.

In the case of resurrection faith, believers rely fundamentally on testimonies from the New Testament. These Easter texts, transmitted through the community, become a living word when 're-presented' through preaching, liturgical 'performance' and personal prayer. Religious music[6] and art also play their role in bringing alive these texts from the New Testament witnesses, who can thus invite us to believe and understand our existence in the light of the crucifixion and resurrection of Christ. Thus Easter witness realises its meaning through being personally appropriated by believers. Like musical compositions, the resurrection texts remain incomplete when not 'performed'. Written by believers and intended to encourage and maintain faith, they fully exist through what we experience in the preaching and sacramental life of the Church. This is the goal of Easter testimony, when it rings true and is confirmed in personal experience within the worshipping community. Ultimately, of course, faith does not reside in Easter texts or in Easter witnesses, but in the risen Jesus and the God who raised him through the power of the Holy Spirit.

Personal Experience of the Risen Christ

A precious saying attributed to Jesus, 'where two or three meet in my name, I shall be there with them' (Matthew 18:20), reflects the experience of early Christians assembled for worship.[7] They experienced the risen Christ's personal presence and the power of his Spirit which 'lifted' them out of themselves and transformed their lives. Christian worship, above all in the Sunday assembly, was and remains the primary home or privileged context in which Easter experience and faith grow and flourish. Christ's death and resurrection is a profound mystery in which we are invited to be totally involved through life and worship, much more than a problem 'out there' to which we might find the answer through the evidence at our disposal. As one who shares Easter faith and Easter worship, I experience the presence of Christ rather than 'observing' it or 'establishing' it through evidence.

Experience in Worship

The setting of liturgy shows how the reality of the resurrection, far from being an 'external' question, is something in which we participate and which 'possesses' us (Philippians 3:12). Believers come together because of the resurrection and around the resurrection. We experience and know together the risen Christ and his victory by sharing in his life, at worship and beyond. Worship is the primary 'place' where people come to believe in the risen Jesus and go on believing in him. Faith results from their prayerful encounter with the living Jesus. In his own ironical fashion Johann Wolfgang von Goethe (1749–1832) illustrates that truth in part one of *Faust*. On Easter Sunday morning Dr Faust is about to commit suicide by drinking poison, when he suddenly hears some church bells ringing out their joy and a choir proclaiming the message of the resurrection. He feels Easter calling him back to life, senses once again the happy faith of his childhood, and gains a brief respite. Goethe, whatever his motives and meaning, reminds us that the risen Christ's presence in the liturgical assembly reaches a special intensity at the climax of Holy Week. The liturgy of Good Friday, with its reading or singing of the passion according to St John, the prayers for all manner of people in their various needs, and the veneration of the cross, evokes the suffering of Christ which continues in the lives of millions of people – in fact, in the lives of everyone.[8] On the following day, the Easter Vigil on Holy Saturday night acts out the community's witness to the resurrection – through readings, prayers, hymns (above all the *Exultet* or Easter Proclamation), symbolic objects (above all, the great Easter Candle), and sacramental signs (in particular, baptism, confirmation and the eucharist).

In many parishes, at the start of Lent or even earlier the RCIA (Rite of Christian Initiation of Adults) offers those who present themselves a process of preparation. They begin their lengthy preparation for baptism with a moving ceremony. A priest traces the sign of the cross on their forehead, ears, eyes, lips, breast and shoulders. In the prayers which accompany these actions the priest asks the candidates to receive the sign of the cross as an expression of Christ's loving and powerful solidarity with them. The candidates may be male or female. They may be young, middle-aged or old. They come from different races, cultures and personal backgrounds. But they all have two things in common with Christ: bodies and sufferings. In that RCIA ceremony, the candidates begin their preparation for baptism by placing under the sign of the cross these two utterly basic features of the human condition.

Then at the Easter Vigil, through their baptism, confirmation, and First Communion, the candidates express the new faith and life which they accept from the risen Christ and his Holy Spirit. At various points in the ceremony they hold in their hands a small taper lit from the tall Easter Candle, so as to dramatise what they receive from the living Christ whom they experience to be present as the Light of the world. The baptistery of a third-century Christian church in Dura Europos (on the right bank of the Euphrates, half way between Aleppo and Baghdad) contains a fresco depicting three women (Mark 16:1–2) carrying torches and moving towards the tomb of Jesus over which rise the stars of morning. This fresco testifies to the link Christians made from the very beginning (Romans 6:3–4) between baptism (and the other sacraments of initiation) and the resurrection. Through baptism, confirmation and the eucharist, the Easter Vigil signifies and effects the initiation of believers into the resurrection.

Day by day, and especially on Sunday, the eucharist dramatises faith in the crucified and risen Christ. This faith, which belongs to the heart of 'the faith that comes to us from the apostles' (First Eucharistic Prayer), has been transmitted from the first century down through the ages to contemporary Catholics and other Christians around the world. The Christian eucharist has secured a liturgical 'succession' of Easter faith. Over the centuries the Easter language, with its accompanying gestures of worship, has not been a 'neutral' conduit which merely reports the experiences of the faithful; it has proved *the* catalyst of fresh Easter experience for each succeeding generation of believers. When, for instance, the people say or sing 'Glory to you, O Lord' before hearing the Gospel read or sung, they acknowledge the risen Jesus present in the text which will be proclaimed and then preached to the assembly. The 'bread of the inspired word' is thus read and 'broken' to announce the resurrection and the presence of Jesus Christ.

The eucharistic acclamations which follow the words of institution express an almost sensory experience of the risen Christ, who is present with his redeeming and life-giving power. The first acclamation ('Christ has died. Christ has risen. Christ will come again.') is a declaration which confesses Easter faith. But the three other acclamations directly address the risen Christ in person:

Dying you destroyed our death, rising you restored our life. Lord Jesus, come in glory.

When we eat this bread and drink this cup, we proclaim your death, Lord Jesus, until you come in glory.

Lord, by your cross and resurrection you have set us free. You are the Saviour of the world.

To summarise, the path to sharing and growing in Easter faith has come by experiencing the risen Christ in worship with others, much more than by analysing evidence in favour of the resurrection. It has been a matter of knowing the risen Christ in direct and lasting experience rather than knowing *things* (the 'relevant' data). No mere mental exercise, Easter faith flourishes in worship – through all that we see, hear, touch, taste, and smell in our experience of the liturgy. This faith also flourishes, one must add, in practice. It enjoys a practical, as well as a liturgical, credibility.

Experience in Life

How does faith work out in practice for those who trust the word of the Easter witnesses and confess the resurrection of Jesus? Here we arrive at ways in which this faith has validated itself in practice by leading believers into a deep union with God and with one another. It has produced and continues to produce creatively good effects in human lives.

Resurrection faith claims not only that Jesus rose from the dead but also that, through the power of the Holy Spirit, he has remained actively present in the world and, in particular, in the lives of Christians. We can find public signs of the permanent and powerful presence of the risen Lord in recognisable examples of holy living. The commitment of individual Christians and of various movements concerned with education, medical care (including care of lepers and those who are HIV positive), and work for people with developmental disabilities, refugees, drug addicts, prisoners and the powerless poor reveal testable, valuable and, at times, heroically productive activity for others. Carried out in the name and through the power of the crucified and risen Jesus, such work suggests his living presence. He 'shows up' in practice when those who know him in faith improve and even transform situations for the crucified of this world and bring hope to those in terrible need. In *Christ the Liberator*, Jon Sobrino reminds us that those who serve the victims of dehumanising forces around the world bring to bear the power and presence of the risen Christ. Sobrino also reminds us that those who serve can draw hope from Christ's presence in the astonishing faith and joy of the victims themselves.[9]

This brings us to the experience of the risen Jesus which recurs in the lives of those who know him in faith. Here the Gospel of John is particularly instructive, inasmuch as it blends two 'horizons', that of the past and that of the present. Through its own version of the baptism of Jesus, his ministry of healing, his miracles (or 'signs', as John calls them), his preaching, his meetings with people in need, his conflicts with religious authorities, his dramatic and messianic entry into Jerusalem, his final meal with the disciples, and the passion, death, and resurrection narratives, the Gospel of John records real events from the past. But, even more than the other three evangelists, John brings out the link between these past events and ongoing experiences of believers or of those who become believers. He blends the horizon of the past with that of the present, so as to reveal how the risen and living Jesus, among other things, shows himself *the* Interpreter and the Transformer of what human beings must typically endure and live through.

John does this by recounting at length encounters between Jesus and people who face recurrent human challenges. Nicodemus brings his religious doubts and difficulties to Jesus (John 3:1–10). The subsequent appearances of Nicodemus in John's Gospel lead us to appreciate the gradual progress he has made after encountering Jesus (John 7:50–52; 19:39–42). John tells at greater length a meeting at a well between Jesus and a Samaritan woman, who has had five husbands and is currently living with someone who is not her husband (John 4:7–42). With consummate tact Jesus engages in dialogue with her and, apparently within a few hours, she is radically changed and becomes the first missionary for Jesus.

The next encounter is prompted by the sickness of a child and the terrible distress which that causes to the boy's father (John 4:46–53). Jesus cures the sick boy, but the healing enjoys a wider impact. The person whose son is cured is introduced as 'a royal official' (vv. 46, 49); then he is called 'the man' or rather 'the human being' (v. 50), and finally 'the father' (v. 53). He enters the story as what he is in public life – an official who carries out a state function. Then he becomes 'the man' who believes the word which Jesus addresses to him. In meeting Jesus he loses, as it were, his public mask. He is simply a human being, face to face with the Lord. He is offered and accepts the only gift which ultimately matters: 'The man believed the word which Jesus spoke to him.' Then he becomes 'the father'. His new faith has not reduced but reinforced his humanity. He is no longer merely an 'official'; but 'the father' who goes back to his family and finds his son restored to health. Then 'all his household' also comes to believe. So far from being a private, isolating force, faith spreads out, and builds communities of faith. What has been just a human household becomes a household of faith.

Someone who is incurable and helpless, a lame man who has been handicapped for 38 years, features next in John's Gospel (John 5:1–18). He cannot move himself and go looking for Jesus, as Nicodemus and the royal official do. In the great crowd of invalids (v. 4) Jesus singles out the one who seems most in need, tries to rouse some hope in him, makes him acknowledge his own helplessness, and cures him: 'Rise, take up your stretcher and walk' (v. 8). But the story of this encounter does not end there. The man is not yet fully healed. As the Gospel subtly puts it, he does not 'know' Jesus (v. 13). Unless he really knows Jesus, he will not be truly saved. Jesus seeks him out, in order to heal him interiorly: 'See, you are well! Sin no more, that nothing worse befall you' (v. 14). Instead of recognising his own sinfulness, coming to know Jesus in faith, and – like the Samaritan woman – spreading that faith, the man becomes unintentionally the first betrayer, a kind of anticipation of Judas in the fourth

Gospel. He goes to those who are outraged that this healing has occurred on the sabbath; he informs them that it is Jesus of Nazareth who has been responsible for the cure. This strengthens their desire to kill Jesus (v. 18). Here for the first time John's Gospel clearly mentions murderous plans to do away with Jesus. This chilling news comes in the aftermath of a loving initiative from Jesus which has succeeded in touching the sick man's body but not his heart. Meeting Jesus and even being physically healed by him do not infallibly and irresistibly transform a human life.

John's Gospel tells, often at considerable length, further stories of encounters in which Jesus interprets and transforms situations: for the man born blind (John 9:1–41); for Martha and Mary when their brother Lazarus died (John 11:1–44); for Mary Magdalene when Jesus himself died and rose (John 19:25; 20:1–2, 11–18); for Peter when he denied even knowing his Master (John 18:15–18, 25–27; 20:3–10; 21:15–19); for Thomas the Twin when he crassly queried the resurrection of Jesus (John 20:24–29). What John provides are typical examples of human struggles and suffering, which take the form of religious doubt (Nicodemus and Thomas), marital breakdown (the Samaritan woman), sickness in the family (the royal official), a permanent handicap (the man lame for 38 years), blindness (the man born blind), a death in the family (Martha and Mary), the loss of someone who is loved very much (Mary Magdalene) and terrible personal failure (Simon Peter). In all these archetypical cases Jesus comes on the scene to interpret some serious challenge and dramatically change the situation. In effect, John's text is saying to us: 'the crucified and risen Jesus lives among us to help us understand what we face and to change what we endure. No matter what our predicament or suffering, he is *the* Interpreter and the Transformer *par excellence*.'

Thus the experiences of life present themselves to believers as the actions of Jesus, who remains powerfully present to interpret and transform whatever it is that they must face. Their Easter faith is nourished by their transformed experiences, which they take to be evidence of his ongoing presence.

Experience through the Holy Spirit

To adapt some words of St Paul (1 Corinthians 12:3), 'no one can say Jesus is risen, except by the Holy Spirit'. The Spirit forms faith in the risen Christ and underpins the claim: 'Jesus is risen and so he is Lord.'

This claim has its background. Just as the Holy Spirit once and for all effected the resurrection of Christ (Romans 8:11), so now the same Spirit makes the risen Christ credible, present and experienced. The inner testimony of the Holy Spirit opens us to accept the 'outer' word of the Easter witnesses and allows us to recognise Christ as present.[10] Hence the Spirit justifies the conclusion: Jesus is present and so he must have been raised from the dead. In this way a past event (the resurrection) is known to ground our present experience, as well as our hopes for the future.

Thus everything hangs together for believers. Their cumulative experience of the risen Christ through his Holy Spirit offers them a coherent, meaningful and truthful vision for worship and life. To adapt the words of Thomas Aquinas quoted at the start of this chapter, each separate experience would not suffice by itself for 'showing perfectly' the presence of the living Christ. Yet all experiences 'taken together establish itself completely'.

I have written this chapter very much as one who grew up with Easter faith and, despite problems experienced at times with lesser items in the creed of Catholic Christianity, has always found belief in the risen Christ to make sense of life in all its complexities and sufferings. This chapter has aimed at sketching what the experience of Easter faith looks and feels like 'from the inside'.

I realise that some may vigorously question the value of religious experience as a guide to truth,[11] in this case as a guide to the truth of the risen Christ's powerful presence in the Church and the world. So be it. Yet it seems thoroughly worthwhile setting out how my experience and that of other Christians has responded to testimony in allowing our Easter faith to be created and developed.

4

The Empty Tomb of Jesus:
History and Theology

If he [Christ] did not rise from the dead, then he
decomposed in the grave like any other man. *He
is dead and decomposed*. In that case he is a teacher
like any other and can no longer *help*; and once
more we are orphaned and alone.

Ludwig Wittgenstein, *Culture and Value*, p. 33c.

For Paul the empty tomb was a self-evident
implication of what was said about the resurrection of Jesus.

Wolfhart Pannenberg, *Systematic Theology*,
vol. 2, p. 359.

T HE FOUR GOSPELS, beginning with Mark 16:1–8, all tell
of Mary Magdalene, either alone (John)[1] or with one (Matthew) or more (Mark and Luke) female companions, discovering
the tomb of Jesus to be open and empty on 'the first day of the
week', the day which later generations were to call the first Easter
Sunday. This New Testament witness raises numerous questions.

Firstly, is it historically reliable or based on events which took
place? Or is the Markan story (and subsequent accounts of the
empty tomb) only a fictional scenario intended to illustrate an
already existing faith in the risen Jesus? In this case the story of
the empty tomb would have come from belief in resurrection
rather than from an independent, historical event which con-

firmed what the appearances established: Jesus had risen from the dead. If the story of the women's discovery on the first Easter morning has no basis in history, was it in the first instance freely composed by Mark himself?[2] Or did Mark 16:1–8 arise from an earlier source, which was itself not based on an historical discovery but was simply a way of illustrating vividly the earliest Christian proclamation of the resurrection (see 1 Corinthians 15:3–5)?[3] A classic difficulty here is that, whereas many scholars accept in general that Mark drew on earlier written and/or oral sources for his passion and resurrection narratives, any particular reconstructions of these sources remain at best tentative and do not command wide scholarly agreement. Finally, there are numerous exegetes who agree with Rudolf Pesch that Mark drew on existing sources for his brief Easter chapter, but who disagree with Pesch by recognising that actual events in history lie behind the tradition or traditions of the women's visit to the tomb.

Secondly, other questions follow from the position we take on the historical origins of the empty tomb story. Would it and how would it affect our faith in the risen Jesus if we were to hold that he lives in glory even though his earthly body quietly decayed in the tomb? A graffito which regularly appears on walls around the world assures its readers: 'There will be no Easter this year. They have found the body.' This graffito implies that such a discovery would destroy Easter faith for many. Seemingly for Ludwig Wittgenstein such a discovery would have ruled out belief in the resurrection.[4] Alternatively, what if we insist that Easter faith does involve something that happened to the body of Christ – i.e. that his corpse disappeared and a glorious being, personally continuous with the dead Jesus, mysteriously appeared? How does this positive 'picture' determine our Easter faith? What does it indicate concerning all that is revealed about God, Jesus himself and our destiny?

The Basis in History

The thesis that the story of the empty tomb in Mark 16:1–8 was totally created by the evangelist himself (see Yarbro Collins in Chapter 2 above) is not plausible. Mark, for all the theological insights in his work that post-World War II scholars have rightly explored, does not, nevertheless, come across as very creative from a literary point of view.[5] Hence it is hardly to be expected that he would invent out of nothing not only an entire episode but also an episode which bore on something of primary importance, the resurrection of Jesus from the dead. Second, the thesis that Mark ends his Gospel with a fictional episode involves us in portraying as gullible Matthew and Luke, who – so the majority of scholars hold – used Mark 16:1–8 as a major source in composing their Easter narratives. Matthew and Luke repeat the main lines of Mark's story as if it were a basically factual narrative. Have they misunderstood Mark? Can a modern scholar evaluate better than the two evangelists the status of their main source? Third, Yarbro Collins 'explains' Mark's composition of the whole passage largely on the basis of Greco-Roman ideas of a notable figure being translated into heaven. Drawing on such motifs, Mark is supposed to have created from nothing his story of Jesus' body being absent from the tomb. We have already seen in Chapter 2 above some of the difficulties in imagining Greco-Roman motifs to have shaped what Mark wrote in his last chapter and in the rest of his Gospel. Various scholars have serious doubts about using such ideas as a master-key for interpreting Mark. Thus Paul Danove, in a literary and rhetorical study of this Gospel, finds little or no evidence of Greco-Roman influence.[6]

What of Pesch's view that Mark, when composing his final chapter, used an earlier tradition about women discovering the tomb of Jesus to be open and empty which was not based on some actual event in history, but was simply a means of illustrating the earliest Christian proclamation of the resurrection which we find classically in 1 Corinthians 15:3–8? Such an argument holds that the tradition behind Mark 16:1–8 and the subsequent empty tomb stories did not convey any factual information about the state of Jesus' tomb. It was simply a way of announcing the resurrection of the crucified Jesus and his subsequent appearances. But can we interpret Mark's final chapter (and the tradition behind it) as merely an imaginative elaboration of what we read in 1 Corinthians 15:3–8? A careful comparison indicates rather, as we saw in Chapter 2 above, that the two traditions (the proclamation of the resurrection and the appearances, on the one hand, and the empty tomb story, on the other) have independent origins.

We are left then with an early tradition which was used by Mark and which does not depend on the message about the resurrection and appearances cited by St Paul – a tradition which tells of some women finding the tomb of Jesus to be open and empty on the first Easter Sunday. This conclusion does not, of course, automatically imply that the empty tomb tradition comes from some actual event in history. Many writers other than Yarbro Collins and Pesch have argued that this tradition does not have a basis in history and offer their own 'explanations'. A good number of these counter-proposals are patently weak and even bizarre.[7] Having concluded that behind Mark 16:1–8 there is a tradition which did not simply develop out of the resurrection/ appearance tradition to *illustrate* the early proclamation of the resurrection, I find only one further hypothesis against the historicity of the empty tomb worth considering: namely, an hypothesis which draws on first-century Jewish beliefs in resurrection.

Those who held such beliefs, for all their differences, always held that the bodies in the graves would be involved when the dead were to be resurrected. That notion of resurrection would have been incompatible with accepting the resurrection of Jesus while admitting that his tomb was not empty and that his body had quietly decayed there. Hence some early, pre-Markan Christians invented the fictional story of three women discovering the tomb of Jesus to be open and empty on 'the first day of the week'. Such Christians:

(1) accepted the personal resurrection of Jesus, yet
(2) knew that his body in the tomb was not involved in that resurrection, but
(3) also knew that others would not accept their proclamation of Jesus' resurrection unless his body buried in the tomb was involved in it, and so
(4) created the story of three women discovering the empty tomb.

Thus they made up this fiction, not to illustrate the message of the resurrection (so Pesch and others), but out of theological necessity.

Notable objections emerge against this hypothesis. First, there is no evidence from first-century Judaism – in particular, Palestinian Judaism – that anyone ever managed to hold together both (1) and (2). Some modern authors have done so, but we have no evidence that any first-century Jews or Christians ever did so: for them, no empty tomb meant no personal resurrection.[8] Second, knowing that Jews, in particular, would not accept the proclamation of the resurrection of Jesus unless his body buried in the tomb were involved in his resurrection, (3), how could any of the first Christians *in Palestine* have made up the story of women discovering the tomb to be empty and managed to succeed with their fiction? At least in and around Jerusalem such a fiction could scarcely have worked; it would too easily have been dismissed as blatantly untrue. Third, the point already made in Chapter 2 above needs to be applied to this present argument. Those concerned to make the proclamation of the resurrection acceptable by including what was a necessary element for first-century Judaism (an empty tomb) and hence theologically driven to create a fictional story about Jesus' empty tomb would have done something strikingly counter-productive by attributing the discovery of his empty tomb to three women. In a culture where women did not count as valid witnesses, they would have credited male disciples with the discovery. Legend-makers do not normally invent positively unhelpful material.

An account of the historical evidence for the empty tomb from Matthew's passion and resurrection narrative could well include a special feature which does not come from Mark: the posting of a guard at the tomb of Jesus (Matthew 27:62–66), and the report and bribing of some members of the guard (Matthew 28:11–14). Matthew states that some of the soldiers were bribed to say that the disciples of Jesus, under the cover of night, stole his body. The evangelist adds: 'This story has been spread among the Jews until this day' (Matthew 28:15). This remark points to Christians and Jews arguing with one another over the tomb of

Jesus at the time when Matthew writes (ca. 80 AD), in a polemic which presupposes that both parties know Jesus' tomb to have been found empty. They agree on this datum which they interpret in radically different ways. Thus Matthew's guard narrative leaves us with the question: given that in around 80 AD Christians and their opponents were in debate over what happened to the body of Jesus, is it still possible to maintain that his remains were still in the tomb and known to be there?[9]

All in all, a reasonable case can be developed for acknowledging an historical core in the Markan tradition of the discovery of the empty tomb (which Matthew and Luke then followed), as well as in the somewhat different Johannine tradition which focuses on Mary Magdalene (John 20:1–2, 11–18). The accounts of Mark and John have a basis in events of history. But what might the empty tomb mean theologically? (a) Does it reveal truth(s) about God which should shape our faith in the risen Jesus? And (b) does it indicate anything about the redemption of human beings and their world brought through the crucified and risen Jesus? These questions must be faced, not least because I suspect that certain difficulties some people have with the empty tomb tradition are more theological than historical – with 'what does it mean?' rather then with 'did it happen?'

Theological Significance

Let me propose some points about the divine self-revelation which are connected with the discovery of the empty tomb. We can then move on to sketch something of the redemptive input of the empty tomb. In both cases let me focus primarily on the oldest account, Mark 16:1–8.

The Divine Self-Revelation

At first glance, the spare eight verses which conclude Mark's Gospel do not look that promising for any theology of divine self-revelation, but these laconic lines prove rich for such a theology. The verses report a pair of elements which persistently shape God's self-revelation: *events* (here the divine action which has already transformed the whole situation before the arrival of the three women) and *words* (here the angelic proclamation). As the Second Vatican Council taught, revelation occurs 'sacramentally' – through the interplay of words and deeds.[10] Moreover, three *contrasts* are built into the story: darkness/light, absence/presence, and silence/speech. They enhance the telling of the episode.

Firstly, Mark's text contrasts not only the darkness of the night (between the Saturday and the Sunday of the resurrection) but also the darkness which enveloped the earth at the crucifixion (Mark 15:33) with the light of the sun which has just risen when the women visit the tomb (Mark 16:2). The three women go to the tomb with light coming into the sky and with something they never imagined about to be revealed: God has definitively overcome darkness and death.

A preliminary hint of what is to be revealed comes when the women 'raise their eyes and see' that the enormous stone, which blocked the entrance to the tomb and their access to the body of Jesus that they intend to anoint, 'has been rolled away' (Mark 16:4). From the 'theological', passive form of the verb the attentive reader knows that God, while not explicitly named, has been at work in bringing about what is humanly impossible – by opening a tomb and raising the dead to new life. The women see the first hint of what God has already done in unexpectedly reversing the situation of death and vindicating the victimised Jesus. Without yet being properly aware of it, the women find themselves confronted with the first disclosure of God's action in the resurrection.

A second contrast emerges once the women enter the tomb itself. The absence of Jesus' body is set over against his personal presence, mediated through an interpreting angel in the form of a well-dressed, 'young man'.

A third contrast pits the confident *words* of the heavenly figure ('He has been raised. He is not here. See the place where they laid him') against the *silence* of the women when they flee from the tomb. Its triple shape adds force to the announcement. The angel proclaims, first, the great truth that concerns everyone and will change the universe for ever: 'He has been raised.' Then he turns to the particular place in which he is addressing the women: 'He is not here.' Finally, he points to the specific spot in the tomb where the body of Jesus had been buried: 'See the place where they laid him.' Both these words of the angel and then the silent flight of the women highlight the dramatic and numinous moment of revelation. Let us see the details.

When the three women enter the tomb, they do not find the body of Jesus but a 'young man, dressed in a white robe, and sitting on the right' (Mark 16:5). His shining apparel is the traditional dress of heavenly messengers. Like the Old Testament figures who remain seated to deliver a judgement, the angel does not rise to greet the women but speaks with authority to deliver a most unexpected message. At the sight of the angel the women respond by being 'greatly amazed' (v. 5) – a reaction which matches the normal biblical response to God's presence in a theophany. After countering their startled reaction with a word of comfort ('do not be amazed') and revealing the resurrection ('he has been raised') (v. 6), the angel commissions them: 'Tell his disciples and Peter that he is going before you into Galilee. There you will see him' (v. 7). But the women 'fled from the tomb. For trembling and astonishment had seized them, and they said nothing to anyone, for they were afraid' (v. 8).

Some commentators, as we saw in note 5 above, explain the silent flight of the three women as their disobedient failure. First of all, the male disciples of Jesus have failed, and now also the women prove to be disobedient failures. They break down and disobey the commission they have received from the angel. So Mark's Gospel is alleged to close with total human collapse.

But is such exegesis rooted in Mark's narrative and does it miss something very important about divine revelation? Does it gloss over the difference between the track record of the male disciples from chapters 6 to 15 and the women's 'track record' in chapters 14, 15 and 16? Beyond question, the male disciples of Jesus start going downhill from Mark 6:52, where the evangelist states that they do not understand the feeding of the five thousand and their hearts 'are hardened'. Their lack of faith then leads Jesus himself to reproach them with their failure to understand and believe (Mark 8:14–21). A little later he reproaches Peter sharply for perpetuating Satan's temptations by refusing to accept the suffering destiny that awaits his Master: 'Get behind me, Satan' (Mark 8:31–33). Then James, John and the other male disciples prove just as thickheaded (Mark 9:32; 10:35–40). Judas betrays Jesus into the hands of his enemies. When their Master is arrested in the Garden of Gethsemane, all the male disciples desert him (Mark 14:50). Peter creeps back and goes into the courtyard of high priest while Jesus is being interrogated. But under pressure he twice denies being a follower of Jesus and then swears that he does not even know Jesus (Mark 14:66–72). None of the male disciples show up at the crucifixion, and it is left to a devout outsider, Joseph of Arimathea, to give Jesus a dignified burial (Mark 15:42–47). The progressive failure of Jesus' male disciples – and, in particular, of the core group of the Twelve – begins at Mark 6:52 and reaches its lowest point in the passion story.

Meanwhile, women have entered Mark's narrative (Mark 14:3–9; 15:40–41, 47). They function faithfully as the men should have done but have failed to do. The women remain true to Jesus right through to the end, and are prepared to play their role in completing the burial rites. The women have 'followed' Jesus and 'ministered' to him in life and in death (Mark 15:41). Does then the frightened silence with which they react to the angel's message express a sudden, unexpected collapse on their part? Those who endorse such a dismal explanation should re-read Mark's Gospel and notice how from the very start (Mark 1:22, 27) people over and over again respond to what Jesus does and reveals with amazement, silence, fear and even terror (for instance, Mark 4:40–41; 6:50–51). His teaching and miracles manifest the awesome mystery of God come personally among us.

In a detailed study Timothy Dwyer has shown how 'wonder' is a characteristic motif in Mark's Gospel and occurs at least 32 times.[11] Comprising 'all of the narrative elements which express astonishment, fear, terror and amazement', it is the appropriate human response to the awesome presence and power of God revealed in the teaching, miracles, death and resurrection of Jesus. Apropos of the three key terms in Mark 16:8, flight, fear and silence, Dwyer appeals to earlier passages in Mark and other relevant texts to show that the terms do not always bear negative connotations. Far from being always defective and the antithesis of faith, 'flight is a common response to confrontation with the supernatural'. The reactions of trembling, astonishment *and fear* in Mark 16:8, as Dwyer shows, 'are consistent with reactions to divine interventions early in the gospel', reactions which 'co-exist with faith' (p. 188, see p. 192). As for 'silence', he illustrates how in biblical stories silence for a time can 'result from a divine encounter' (p. 189). The silence of the three women is best understood as provisional: in due time they spoke to the disciples (p. 192). The women remained silent with inappropriate persons, 'until their message could be passed on to the appropriate audience, the disciples'.[12]

To sum up, it is with flight, trembling, astonishment, silence and fear that the women initially receive the angel's message about God's action in raising Jesus (Mark 16:6) and about Jesus' appearance(s) to take place in Galilee (Mark 16:7). But these are proper reactions to the climax of divine revelation which has occurred in the resurrection of the crucified Jesus. God's action has transformed the whole situation. The women have experienced the death of Jesus (Mark 15:40–41) and his burial (Mark 15:47); they expect to find a crucified corpse when they visit the tomb. Their intense response to the angel's words matches the awesome power of God, now disclosed in that 'which is greater and indeed sums up all the other acts in the gospel' of Mark.[13] God has triumphed over evil, the divine kingdom is breaking into the world, and the victimised Jesus is known to have been finally vindicated as the Son of God (Mark 1:1, 11; 9:7; 15:39).[14]

In Mark's Gospel the crucifixion and resurrection stand against each other. But they interpret and 'reveal' each other and may never be separated. Mark exemplifies this mutual 'illumination' through two juxtaposed statements which the interpreting angel makes to the three women: 'You are looking for Jesus of Nazareth who was crucified' and 'He has been raised' (Mark 16:6).

To that message of the resurrection of the crucified One the women react appropriately.

Read this way, Mark's concluding eight verses yield a rich commentary on the divine self-revelation conveyed by the numinous wonder of the resurrection. The later Gospels of Luke and John were to fill out the picture of the divine revelation at the resurrection by highlighting the outpouring of the Holy Spirit. Matthew, albeit discreetly, also does so by associating the formula of baptism 'in the name of the Father, and of the Son, *and of the Holy Spirit* with the post-resurrection rendezvous of Jesus with 'the eleven disciples' (Matthew 28:16–20). Thus Matthew, Luke and John press beyond the Easter revelation of the Father and the Son (found in Mark 16) to acknowledge the full, 'trinitarian' disclosure of Father, Son and Holy Spirit.

Redemption through Christ

What God reveals changes the situation. As the Old Testament prophets insist, the revealing word of God is effective and transforming (for instance, Isaiah 55:10–11). Revelation and redemption can be distinguished but never separated. Mark's empty tomb narrative also exemplifies this truth, by presenting or at least hinting at some major aspects not only of revelation but also of God's redeeming activity. At least three points merit retrieval.

(1) God, while never formally named in the eight verses of Mark's concluding chapter, has triumphed over the evil and injustice which struck Jesus down. Glorious new life and not death have the final word. Two verbs in the passive voice point to the divine activity which utterly transforms the situation established by the crucifixion and burial of Jesus. The link between the crucified Jesus and the risen Jesus is the victorious power of God. The great stone blocking the entrance to the tomb 'has been rolled away', and one understands 'by God'; Jesus himself 'has been raised', and one understands 'by God'. Even before the women arrive, the divine power has dramatically reversed the situation of death and injustice.

Matthew and Luke will picture the victorious and liberating divine action of the resurrection in a fuller context, by adding, for instance, 'inclusive' elements: the saving divine action at the start of their Gospels matches the Easter action at the end. We will take this up in the next chapter.

(2) Many commentators find a firm hint of redemptive rehabilitation in the angel's words to the women: 'Tell his disciples and Peter that he is going before you into Galilee. There you will see him' (Mark 16:7). The male disciples sinfully failed when Jesus was arrested. They fled into the night and never showed their faces at the crucifixion and burial of Jesus. Peter denied that he even knew Jesus. But now their failure is forgiven, and their discipleship is to be restored when they meet their risen Lord in Galilee. Using the promise to be conveyed to the male disciples, Mark hints at the way in which redemption involves the reconciliation of sinners. The other evangelists – and, in particular, John – have more to say about this reconciliation, as we shall see in the next chapter.

(3) Then the angelic figure in the tomb offers a subtle hint of the redemptive power of love. Almost inevitably attentive readers of Mark's Gospel, when they come to the 'young man dressed in white' (*stole* in Greek; Mark 16:5), recall another 'young man' who left his 'linen cloth' (*sindon* in Greek) in the hands of those who had come to arrest Jesus and fled naked into the night (Mark 14:51–52). In chapter 14 the nakedness of the young man, the linen shroud, and the darkness of the night readily evoke the sense of Jesus now being led away defenceless and facing imminent death and burial. Three days later a 'young man' clothed at dawn in the white robe of resurrection also symbolises what has happened to Jesus, who has been executed, buried in a 'linen cloth' (*sindon*; Mark 15:46), and raised gloriously from the dead. The shroud of death has given way to the shining robe of resurrection.

The Markan 'young man' of the death and resurrection narratives serves as a symbolic counterpart for Jesus himself. He also personifies some aspects of redemptive love. Here I go beyond any conscious intentions of the evangelist himself. But there is a 'plus value' in his text which opens itself to several reflections on how the divine love works to save us.[15] I feel encouraged to do so by a feature not only of Mark but also of Matthew and Luke. These three Gospel writers never explicitly report Jesus as saying that his heavenly Father has *agape* or love for human beings, and rarely attribute to Jesus himself the explicit language of love (in Mark only at 10:21 and 12:30–31). Yet the universal kindness and mercy of God (e.g. Matthew 5:45; Luke 6:35–36) and Jesus' compassionate care for the sick, the sinful, and the lost make no sense, if we do not recognise how love motivates and empowers the whole story in the Synoptic Gospels. The fact that the articulation of redemption in terms of love remains largely implicit earlier in Mark's Gospel prompts me to articulate the redeeming love of God implied in the final chapter.

First, the angelic messenger shows divine love through accepting and affirming the three startled women. To love others is to approve of them, and God's redemptive love means a fundamental divine approval of our 'being there'. Through the angelic 'young man', God expresses such affirming, loving approval of the three women and of those to whom they are to bring the wonderful message of the resurrection. If we agree that love most radically means approval, we find such approving love of God embodied in Mark's Easter chapter.

Second, love entails active good will towards the other. The angel takes the initiative in reaching out to the three women, and with a benevolent and practical concern for their welfare shares with them the good news of the resurrection which will change for ever their life and that of the other disciples of Jesus. This gift of love will become the self-gift of love, when they keep the rendezvous in Galilee ('there you will see *him*') and meet the risen Jesus himself. The divine giving will then become the self-gift of the Son of God in person.

In all situations, love as gift includes also a trusting disclosure. When we make a gift of ourselves, we do so also by revealing ourselves to those whom we love. This third element is suggested by the angel's promise 'there you will *see* him'. The risen Jesus will make himself available and visible to them. That promised self-disclosure will redemptively transform their existence.

Fourth, love as gift does not merely bless and bestow value on those who already exist; it brings them into existence. In what begins with the women's encounter in the tomb, divine love is starting to bring about a new creation. The women and then the men will be created anew. In his love Christ is going to bless them for ever with a new and definitive identity and relationship through him to his Father.

Authentic love puts those who love at risk – a fifth dimension of love which can be retrieved from Mark's spare account. The angelic messenger recognises that the women are looking for 'Jesus of Nazareth, *who was crucified*'. The saving love of Christ, like all generously authentic love, has made him vulnerable, cost him much and even put him on a cross. In various languages a wise choice calls Jesus' suffering and death his 'passion' – a term which combines intense love with the mortal suffering it brought the lover. Second to none in its dramatic intensity, Mark's passion story tracks the steadfastness of Jesus' commitment that made him vulnerable right to the end, even when one of his male disciples betrayed him, another denied him, and the rest fled in terror. The terrible suffering which his self-forgetful love cost him is evoked and recalled when Mark's text identifies Jesus as he 'who was crucified'.

Reciprocity comes up as a sixth item which an account of redemptive love can find implied in Mark's Easter story. Without such reciprocity love remains radically incomplete, a 'disinterested' love which is at best a kind of unilateral generosity or outgoing beneficence. A giving without receiving, even more a giving that deliberately excludes any possibility of receiving and reciprocal transformation, can hardly be deemed love. Love is an essentially relational reality.[16] Love of its nature aims to establish and maintain in mutual freedom a relationship. To express love is in effect to hope that this love will be returned, but not in a selfish fashion which simply exploits the other to fulfil my needs and yield me some desired benefits. Whenever the openness and desire for a reciprocal relationship and a mutual giving and receiving is missing, one must wonder whether the lover deals with the beloved as a personal agent and respects the integrity of the other. As Vincent Bruemmer observes, we find our very identity in the mutual relationship of love: 'Our identity as persons' is not determined by ourselves alone, but is 'bestowed on us in the love which others have for us . . . Our identity is equally determined by the love we have for others. In both senses we owe our identity as persons to others.'[17]

The reciprocity that belongs essentially to God's redeeming love repeatedly surfaces in Jesus' ministry, when he invites others to committed discipleship (e.g. Mark 10:21). He desires a loving relationship with others, but treats them all as free agents. Their redeemed identity as persons will be bestowed upon them in the love which he has for them and the love by which they respond to him. In Mark's closing chapter the risen Christ invites his disciples to keep a rendezvous with him in Galilee. Mark's readers know that they will freely keep that rendezvous and thus find their lasting identity in a mutual relationship of love with the risen Christ.

A seventh characteristic of God's redeeming love shows up, albeit briefly, in the final eight verses of Mark's Gospel: the divine beauty which rouses our love and so transforms us. This is a theme made familiar by the *Confessions* (10. 27) of St Augustine.[18] At present the divine beauty of the risen Lord which stirs our love remains mysterious, and is revealed only indirectly. In the final chapter of Mark that indirect revelation of his saving beauty occurs through the presence of the angelic messenger. As we shall see in the next chapter, Matthew takes a hint from Mark and presents more robustly the brilliant and powerful angelic beauty which transmutes a situation of death into one of redeemed life. But something is already there in the youth and beauty of God's messenger whom we meet in Mark's empty tomb story. In his own discreet way the 'young man', who serves as a double for Jesus, vindicates the truth of Dostoevsky's dictum that 'beauty will save the world'.

Such then are seven aspects of redeeming love which can be

gleaned from Mark's final chapter: the divine approval; the gift of God's love which will become a self-gift when the disciples 'see' Jesus; the disclosure of the risen Jesus which will transform the lives of the disciples; the new creation which the resurrection brings; the vulnerable love of Jesus which has effected this new situation; the reciprocity of love to be found in the lasting relationship which the disciples will form with Jesus; his risen, divine beauty which will transform their lives.

In reflecting thus on the last chapter of Mark's Gospel, I have hoped to bring out its rich treasure of thought for those who want to move beyond merely historical arguments about the empty tomb of Jesus and catch something of its theological significance now. Mark's narrative creates possible ways of understanding divine revelation and human redemption. In the next and final chapter I plan to show how the other Gospels have even more to suggest about what the story of the empty tomb symbolises and conveys in terms of divine revelation and redemption.

A Coda: On Going Beyond the Literal Meaning

Let me begin by stating that I firmly agree with the need for an historical-critical approach to the Gospels, which recognises three stages in the development of our canonical texts: the stage of Jesus himself; the stage of (largely oral) transmission in the early Christian communities; and the final stage in the work of the evangelists themselves (first Mark, then Matthew and Luke, and finally John – to use the traditional names). At the third level, the historical-critical method (which, despite talk of 'the' method, is not monolithic) attempts to establish precisely what the evangelist intended to express (i.e. the literal meaning of the text).

Analysing a Gospel within its original historical context, remembering the literary and religious conventions of the time, examining the ways such a later evangelist as Matthew seems to have drawn on Mark, on a collection of sayings traditionally named Q (apparently used independently by Matthew and Luke), and on other sources (both oral and possibly written), and investigating the motives and interests which probably led Matthew to write can help determine the literal meaning or what the evangelist intended in particular passages to convey to his readers in around 80 AD. Even if Matthew never documented his intentions through letters or a diary which might be available for us, we can still reach reasonably-argued conclusions about what he intended to say. At the same time, of course, where his Gospel introduced symbolic language of parables and traditional apocalyptic warnings, we must beware of thinking that what he wrote meant 'just this'; that is to say, we must avoid thinking that there was always only one literal meaning to be established. Parabolic and apocalyptic language cannot be pinned down to just one meaning. The evangelist himself may well have been aware of the symbolic nature of that language and never intended merely one meaning. Add too the fact that ancient, as well as modern, writers can write with a deliberate ambiguity, which is open to several meanings.

All that said, it is truly valuable to use historical-critical techniques to pursue the literal meaning of Gospel texts: for instance, of Jesus' response to the disciple (not named here) who drew his sword and struck at one of those who came to arrest his Master: 'he who takes the sword will perish by the sword' (Matthew 26:52). In the immediate context of the Matthean account of the betrayal of Jesus (stage three), this proverbial saying provides one of three reasons for rejecting violence; it also reflects the preference for non-violence found much earlier in the Gospel (Matthew 5:38–42). The proverb may reflect something of a second stage: the experience and convictions of the Matthean community who had survived the awful violence of the Jewish-Roman war (66–70 AD). One can also argue that the proverb goes back to Jesus, from whom other sayings about non-violence also seem to derive (stage one). In any case the literal meaning about not 'taking the sword' seems clear: those who employ violence will be destroyed by it.[19]

On a visit to Verdun in 1967, what Matthew wrote took on fresh meaning for me when I looked at the fortifications and trenches pulverised in the ferocious shelling of 1916 and then stopped to pray in several cemeteries. One cemetery alone con-

THE EMPTY TOMB OF JESUS: HISTORY AND THEOLOGY

tained over 300,000 small white crosses. At Verdun violence destroyed the lives of over a million French and German soldiers who took up – or in many cases were forced to take up – not swords but rifles, machine guns and artillery pieces. In the twentieth century, as very often before, so-called Christian nations failed to hear the words from Matthew's Gospel and tragically continued to illustrate the self-destructiveness of violence. The evangelist could not possibly have anticipated the many wars Christian nations were to fight down through the centuries, let alone thought of modern trench warfare and the mass use of high explosives. His proverb about non-violence is literally addressed to an individual and about individuals who resort to violence; yet, when re-read and re-considered in a twentieth-century war cemetery, it carries a fresh freight of meaning and truth.

At the same time, what the proverb can mean to someone in the context of the twentieth or early twenty-first century maintains some continuity with the meaning the evangelist intended in the first century. The way in which his text can be re-actualised and come alive in modern times is not simply alien to his original meaning; there is continuity in discontinuity.

In a similar way scrutinising the Easter texts of the four evangelists for meaning and truth in the areas of revelation and redemption does not mean manipulating those texts and making them mean just about anything we want them to mean. Whether we like it or not, we read those texts after two thousand years of Christian reflection on the nature of redemption, of worship through which Christians experienced themselves to be blessed with the fruits of Christ's redeeming work, and of discipleship in which uncounted numbers of disciples aspired to live lives worthy of their Redeemer. In the last three hundred years issues of meaning and truth have made questions of God's self-revelation more crucial than ever for official teachers, theologians and other Christians. Inevitably those who read today the Easter texts bring to them questions, experiences and meanings which have accumulated over two thousand years and which play their proper role when those texts are 're-actualised' in modern contexts. The original, literal meanings intended by the evangelists, to the extent to which these can be established, remain an essential, normative point of reference. But we cannot be satisfied with merely establishing such original meanings (or fondly thinking we are establishing such meanings) and leaving it at that. The texts, once composed and distributed by the evangelists, began to have a life of their own. The understanding, interpretation and application of their texts were never rigidly limited by what the original authors intended to convey in writing for their particular audiences.

What I propose here echoes, of course, what many philosophers, literary critics and others have long ago spelled out. Once any text is written and published, it begins to have its own history when people in different situations read and interpret it. Whether it is novel, a poem, a political constitution or, I would add along with many others, a biblical book, it sets up on its own and can mean and communicate to its readers more than its author(s) ever consciously knew or intended. In short, the meanings of such texts consistently go beyond the literal sense intended by the original authors. When reviewing a life of Miguel de Cervantes (1547–1616), A. J. Close strikingly showed how what is arguably the world's greatest literary classic, *Don Quixote*, 'has managed to present a new facet to each succeeding age'.[20]

This coda has aimed at justifying, albeit briefly, the search for new facets about revelation and redemption in, or at least on the basis of, the Easter texts of the Gospels. When doing that, provided we constantly keep in mind what the evangelists originally intended or at least hinted at, we will not indulge in unchecked, wild flights of theological fancy. To insist doggedly on the original, literal meaning alone would mean 'having' the original text but 'missing' a rich range of valuable meanings to which in the course of history it has continued to give birth.[21]

5

Easter As Revelation and Redemption: Matthew, Luke and John

Simon, son of John, do you love me?

John 21:15, 16, 17

To believe in God the Father almighty means . . . to believe in the omnipotence of love and in love's eschatological victory over hatred, violence and egoism. It entails the duty of living *by* this omnipotence and *for* this victory.

Walter Kasper, *The God of Jesus Christ*, p. 157

Our identity as persons is bestowed on us in the love which others have for us . . . Our identity is equally determined by the love we have for others. In both senses we owe our identity as persons to others.

Vincent Bruemmer, *The Model of Love*, p. 171

THIS CHAPTER WILL PRESS BEYOND the previous chapter's development of the themes of the revealing and saving activity of God. It can do so by going further than the eight verses of the Markan Easter story in which there is no appearance of the risen Jesus but simply a promise that he will appear in Galilee. Matthew's final chapter contains 20 verses and reports two appearances of Jesus. Luke's Easter chapter runs to 53 verses and also reports two appearances, with a hint of a third (Luke 24:34). Finally, John's Gospel contains two Easter chapters, which relate four appearances of the risen Christ. In comparison with Mark's closing chapter, we can glean more from Matthew, Luke and John when we reflect on the revelation and redemption brought by the resurrection of the crucified Jesus. Using their stories is a valuable way of developing a narrative approach to the two distinguishable but inseparable dimensions of God's self-communication: revelation and redemption.

Revelation

The divine self-disclosure is strikingly strengthened in Matthew, Luke and John by the fact that the risen Jesus appears *and speaks*. His words elucidate the significance of the revelation effected through his resurrection from the dead. In Chapter 2, we examined briefly the Easter appearances which Paul reports. When doing so (1 Corinthians 9:1; 15:3–8; Galatians 1:12, 16), the Apostle does not mention any words of the risen Lord. What then of the words attributed to the risen Christ by Matthew, Luke and John?

A careful comparison shows how the words of the risen Christ in one Gospel enjoy few, and then only approximate, parallels in the other two Gospels. In the Easter narratives we find nothing like the close and extensive parallelisms characteristic of the words of Jesus reported in the accounts of his ministry from Mark, Matthew and Luke. Moreover, in Matthew, Luke and John the language of the risen Jesus is heavily stamped with the characteristics of each particular evangelist. Matthew, for example, concludes his Gospel with what looks like his own formulation: 'All authority in heaven and on earth has been given to me. Go therefore and make disciples of all nations, baptising them in the name of the Father and of the Son and of the Holy Spirit, teaching them to observe all that I have commanded you; and behold, I am with you always, to the close of the age' (Matthew 28:18–20). These words take up language and summarise themes of this Gospel in a way which makes the section 'a climax and conclusion of Matthew's particular presentation of the gospel material and of the figure of Christ, and which would make it as out of place at the end of any other gospel as it is completely in place here'.[1] When concluding his Gospel, Matthew both cites the trinitarian baptismal formula used by Christians of his day and echoes their faith in the exalted Christ's presence which they experience vividly at their liturgical assemblies (see also Matthew 18:20).

What then should be said about the origin and status of the words attributed to the risen Jesus? Matthew, Luke and John all knew that, in the longer term if not immediately, through his post-resurrection appearances Christ initiated a mission to the world. In their own ways and using traditions (other than Mark 16:1–8) available to them, they articulated the mission-inaugurating function of the Easter encounters and what the mission involved (e.g. baptism and the forgiveness of sins) by attributing appropriate words to the risen Jesus. To say this is to indicate the probable origin of these words and not to challenge their truth and value for illuminating what the resurrection dis-closes and what the risen Christ in effect communicated to his apostolic witnesses.

In the various resurrection narratives the theme of revelation (through words and events) surfaces repeatedly, as does the con-viction that divine help must be available before human beings can perceive God's supreme disclosure in the resurrection of Christ. Let us see how such help is pictured, for instance, in Matthew's story. Here the Angel of the Lord functions to suggest that the truth conveyed lies beyond the reach of ordinary observa-tion. The women can see the empty tomb where Jesus' body had been laid, but they need to hear the angelic word if they are to grasp the revelation which the empty tomb entails. A few verses later, Matthew remarks that at the rendezvous on a mountain in Galilee, the eleven disciples become aware of a presence. Some recognise (and worship) at once their risen Lord, while others remain irresolute and doubtful (Matthew 28:17). Christ must draw near and speak, before they all know perfectly well who he is and what their mission is to be. On the sacred mountain of revelation the risen Lord commissions his followers to preach, baptise and teach. Matthew directs our attention fairly firmly to what *was* revealed through the resurrection of the crucified Jesus and through the once-and-for-all encounters with him.

Luke and John, however, show a richer and more obvious interest in the ongoing revelatory experience of the risen Lord. This will occur above all in the liturgy. Repeatedly the Easter texts of Luke and John state or at least imply that the risen Jesus is to be personally experienced in:

(1) the eucharist,
(2) meal fellowship,
(3) the forgiveness of sins,
(4) the reading, hearing and reception of scripture,
(5) the dynamic operation of the Holy Spirit, and
(6) the experience of faith.

The two evangelists point to these elements of Christian worship and life which signal Christ's continuing and effective presence in his Church. Let us see how themes and hints in Luke and John help us to fill out a post-resurrection vision of revelation.

(1) In 'the breaking of the bread' the two disciples at Emmaus find their eyes opened and they know their risen Lord (Luke 24:30–31, 35). The eucharistic overtones are unmistakable. Christians, Luke implies, will grasp the risen Christ's presence when they gather for the eucharist.

(2) Closely allied with those times are their experiences of the Lord when they meet for meals and/or worship. He reveals himself when they gather in his name (Luke 24:33–43; John 20:19–23). At breakfast together on the lakeside the disciples 'know' that 'it is the Lord' (John 21:12–13).

(3) John explicitly connects the forgiveness of sins with the presence of the risen Christ on Easter Sunday evening (John 20:23). He suggests this connection in other ways as well. Earlier on the first Easter Sunday something more than a mere physical movement seems implied, when John portrays Mary Magdalene as 'turning around' and then 'turning' (John 20:14, 16) before she can recognise the risen Christ. The

discernment that brings faith in the risen Christ who is revealed involves 'conversion'. This holds true of the 'third time that Jesus was *manifested* to the disciples after he was raised from the dead' (John 21:14). Peter's meeting with the risen Christ becomes the occasion of forgiveness for the disciple who has three times denied his Master. Thus at several points in his Easter narrative John transmits to his readers the conviction: 'Wherever you experience the forgiveness of sins, there you can experience the risen Christ to be present and revealed to you.'

(4) Luke clearly links this presence and disclosure with the revelation mediated through scripture. The two disciples on the Emmaus road are offered and accept a new perspective on the biblical witness as they move towards acknowledging Christ's presence (Luke 24:13–32). Back in Jerusalem, the risen Christ enables his followers to perceive how the scriptures testify to and reveal him as the one who must suffer and enter into his glory (Luke 24:44–47).

(5) John 20:22 and Luke 24:49 obviously point to the operation of the Holy Spirit as manifesting the effective presence of the risen Lord. Where the Spirit and the Spirit's gifts are received, there the risen Christ is revealed and at work.

(6) Finally, John implies that where men and women confess Christ as 'my Lord and my God,' there Christ, albeit invisibly, meets them. Hence the fourth evangelist, unlike Luke, concludes the body of his Gospel without a farewell scene or the narrative of an ascension, and leaves Jesus' words ringing in his readers' ears: 'Blessed are those who have not seen and yet believe' (John 20:29). They are blessed who believe in and experience the risen Christ, who – even if he remains invisible – is truly present and disclosed to them.

Thus in various ways the Lukan and Johannine Easter narratives draw their readers' attention to the lasting disclosure of the risen Christ's presence. For his part Matthew, albeit more briefly, also alerts us to this presence through the promise, 'I am with you always, to the close of the age.' This is a presence which will be manifested and mediated – so Matthew implies – through the worldwide mission, the administration of baptism, and the teaching which transmits Jesus' 'commandments' (Matthew 28:19–20).

Redemption

I have just been developing a *narrative* approach, through which themes concerned with the divine self-disclosure can be gleaned from the final chapters to Matthew, Luke and John. The Gospels satisfy our human appetite for narrative. But they do not merely aim to satisfy our desire to find out 'what happened next'. By mulling over the texts and their hints of God's self-revelation, readers can begin to glimpse 'what it was all about'. The Easter chapters by Matthew, Luke and John also let us glimpse 'what it was all about' from three redemptive points of view: the divine victory over evil and injustice, the reconciliation of sinners, and love.

The Victory of Life

In his Easter story Matthew draws a large contrast between Jesus' friends (merely two women, Mary Magdalene and 'the other Mary') and the violent and hostile forces of injustice (represented by a group of soldiers set to guard the tomb). The evangelist skilfully shifts focus from the two women who witness the burial of Jesus and mourn at his grave (Matthew 27:61), to the stationing of the guard (Matthew 27:62–66), back to the women who on Easter Sunday come after dawn to visit the grave (Matthew 28:1), again to the soldiers who at the sight of the Angel of the Lord 'become like dead men' (Matthew 28:4), and then back again to the women who receive the Easter news (Matthew 28:5–7).

Against the unjust powers of this world, represented by the squad of soldiers, those who stand with Jesus seem helpless. Pontius Pilate and the chief priests have sealed the tomb of Jesus and set a guard to watch over it. There is to be no monkey business. Through the power of the Roman Empire and the religious establishment in Jerusalem, Jesus is dead and buried.

His corpse lies in a tomb that is sealed and guarded. Nothing more can happen. His body is locked away and will quietly decay. But then through the magnificent 'Angel of the Lord', God acts to change dramatically the whole situation, vindicate Jesus (and the two women), and shift the balance of power. The soldiers, in a stroke of delicious irony, become themselves like helpless corpses. They thought that they were guarding a dead body. Now it is they who fall to the ground and become themselves 'like dead men'.

The two women run to share with the male disciples of Jesus the astonishing truth of the resurrection and on their way have the unique joy of meeting the risen Jesus himself (Matthew 28:8–10). Meanwhile some of the guard go into Jerusalem and report to the religious authorities 'everything that has happened'. These members of the guard are then paid handsomely to spread a false story about the fate of Jesus' body. They are bribed to say: 'His disciples came by night and stole the body while we were asleep' (Matthew 28:11–15). This cover up in Matthew's resurrection narrative recalls some elements in an episode at the beginning of the passion narrative, when the chief priests and elders plot the death of Jesus. They offer money to Judas in return for betraying his Master (Matthew 26:3–4, 15). Those opposed to Jesus symbolise *death*, *treachery* and *lies*, whereas the two faithful women receive and announce the amazing *truth* of his new *life*. The friends of God may feel themselves to be weak and helpless like the holy women opposed to the apparently overwhelming might of a great political power. But God can and will redemptively change everything and prove victorious over evil.

Thus a large pattern links the concluding chapters from Matthew. It speaks of the power and life of God, who protects and vindicates not only his Son but also the two women who represent faithful discipleship. This pattern at the end of Matthew's Gospel recalls something similar at the beginning – an example of inclusion.

Matthew's story of Herod the Great, the visit of the Magi, the death of the Holy Innocents, and the flight of the Holy Family into Egypt (Matthew 2:1–18) shows how the coming of Jesus makes it possible for us to hope that God will bring stunning reversals in situations of sinful horrors. There may have been worse tyrants than Herod, but few have equalled, let alone surpassed, his ruthless standard of vicious brutality. Without doubt he deserves a place on the shortlist of the ugliest despots in history. Within his own family circle he murdered his favourite wife and three of his sons. At home and beyond he dealt out death, and so prompted the bitter comment from the Roman Emperor, Augustus Caesar: 'Better to be Herod's pig than Herod's son.'

A treacherous and cunning man, Herod plays true to form when the Magi call on him. He tries to trick them into revealing the identity and location of the child born to be King of the Jews, on the pretext of wanting to pay his own homage to the baby. Possessed by paranoid fear, he cannot tolerate the thought of a possible rival, and orders the massacre of all the baby boys in and around Bethlehem. Those painters who have depicted this slaughter bring out the hatred and wickedness that motivate the killing.

Matthew's story features a key figure in an 'Angel of the Lord' (Matthew 2:13), the agent of God in saving the Holy Family. God also acts to warn and save the Magi. Those who stand obediently with God in the story – Mary, her child, Joseph and the Magi – seem utterly weak and defenceless against the power of a wicked tyrant. But God effortlessly changes the situation and saves them. The figure of the 'Angel of the Lord', who also comes on the scene shortly before and after (Matthew 1:20–25; 2:19–20), turns up in Matthew's Gospel only here at the beginning and then, much later, at the end (Matthew 28:2–7).

For all time Herod represents death, lies, hatred and wickedness. The Christ Child (at the start of Matthew's Gospel) and the risen Jesus (at the end of the Gospel) reverse all that, by overcoming death with life, lies with truth, hatred with love, and wickedness with God's gracious goodness. Both at the beginning and at the end, the Angel of the Lord helps us to acknowledge what God is doing in bringing about the redeeming victory of life.

Without abandoning the language of resurrection (Luke 24:7), Luke shows a particular liking for the language of victorious life. At the tomb of Jesus the two interpreting angels who speak with one voice challenge the party of women: 'Why do you seek the living among the dead?' (Luke 24:5). Then at the heart of the Emmaus story, this challenge is recalled by the two disciples. They tell the mysterious stranger about a vision of angels who told the women: 'he is alive' (Luke 24:23). This language of life in the Easter context is not a Lukan monopoly; other New Testament authors apply it to the risen Jesus (e.g. Romans 14:9; Revelation 1:18). Nevertheless, the explicit use of this language sets Luke's Easter chapter apart from the Easter chapters of the other evangelists.

Since Luke's primary audience was probably Gentile rather than Jewish, this may have been one of his reasons for introducing alongside the language of resurrection that of life. The terminology of life, which is in any case biblical, could communicate better with non-Jewish readers. It continues to do so today. For some years I have been fascinated by the frequent use which modern advertising makes not only of certain images of life but also of the explicit language of life. When I was leaving Rome in mid-October 2002 to deliver the Martin D'Arcy Lectures for Campion Hall (Oxford University), I spotted a large advertisement for a brand of mobile phones ('Live without frontiers') and another for a TV pay channel which specialises in sport ('Live the legend'). Both messages were accompanied, respectively, by a picture of a lively young woman and of a vigorous young male athlete. Once arrived in Oxford, I made my way to Blackwell's and bought a couple of books. I was delighted to read on the plastic bag which the shop assistant gave me: 'Live life. Buy the book.' Two thousand years ago Luke chose a word which clearly continues to communicate well.

In any case Luke may have had other reasons for using the language of life. It sets out the present situation of Jesus: he has been raised from the dead and therefore he is victoriously alive. Life represents the permanent condition into which the resurrection has brought Jesus. Moreover, 'life' suggests very well what

Jesus wishes to share with us here and hereafter; he is risen from the dead in order that we might live in God now and for ever.[2]

Before leaving what Luke contributes to this first way of understanding the redemptive impact of the resurrection, we can reflect on two themes which may go beyond his conscious intentions but which, nevertheless, find a foothold in his text. First, the *emptiness* of the tomb as a kind of reverse symbol indicates the *fullness* of life into which the risen Jesus has gone. Graves naturally suggest the quiet decay of an existence dissolved by death. The empty tomb of Jesus symbolises the opposite, the complete life which has overcome the silence of death.

Second, angels turn up at the beginning and the end of Luke's Gospel (Luke 1:5–22, 26–38; 2:8–14; 24:4–7, with possibly an angel in 22:43), along with other such elements as the stress in chapters 1—2 and 24 on events being 'in accordance with the scriptures'. An angelic presence forms an 'inclusion' which links the opening and the close of this Gospel, and in particular associates the virginal conception and birth of Jesus in chapters 1 and 2 with his being raised from the grave in chapter 24.[3] A unique divine initiative brought about his being conceived in the womb of a virgin, even as a similar initiative brought it about that he emerged gloriously alive from the tomb-womb. By associating angels not only with the conception and birth of Jesus but also with his rising from the grave, Luke's text hints at the parallel between the earthly life into which Jesus came from Mary's womb and the heavenly life into which he rose from the tomb. This is one comment prompted by the evangelist's use of angels in an 'inclusion'.

The Reconciliation of Sinners
All four Gospels indicate how the passion and crucifixion of Jesus uncovers the nature of sin. But the Easter chapters of Matthew, Luke and John, even more than that of Mark, have also something to contribute to a sense of the resurrection of Jesus effecting the reconciliation of sinners with God and with one another. By inserting what was to become the lasting baptismal formula in his final chapter (Matthew 28:19), Matthew embodied the forgive-

ness of sins in the context of Jesus' resurrection from the dead. At the start of his Gospel, he had told of John baptising in the Jordan those who confessed their sins and announcing the coming of the One who would baptise 'with the Holy Spirit and fire' (Matthew 3:1–12). The ministry of John the Baptist prefigured the definitive ministry of the followers of Jesus, who were to baptise for the forgiveness of sins and 'in the name of the Father, and of the Son, and *of the Holy Spirit*' (Matthew 28:19). In the brief final scene on a mountain in Galilee, Matthew presupposed the outpouring of the Holy Spirit and the reconciliation of sinners who were to come from all nations and become the disciples of the risen Christ.

In his Easter chapter Luke has the risen Jesus announcing that in his name 'repentance for the forgiveness of sins is to be proclaimed to all nations.' This promise is associated with the coming of the Holy Spirit (Luke 24:47–48). The promise is fulfilled at Pentecost when the outpouring of the Spirit occurs and Peter invites the crowd (who represent all nations) to accept reconciliation with God: 'Repent and be baptised, every one of you, in the name of Jesus the Messiah for the forgiveness of sins; then you will receive the gift of the Holy Spirit' (Acts 2:38). This baptism for the forgiveness of sins gathers believers from all nations into the new community which emerges at Pentecost. The gathering of repentant sinners, which completes the resurrection and the coming of the Spirit, has been exquisitely foretold in the words of John about the death of Jesus 'gathering into one the children of God who have been scattered' (John 11:52).

To gather human beings, who have been alienated from God and from one another, includes and goes beyond the forgiveness of sins to prove itself a pre-eminent work of love. Matthew, Luke and, even more, John help us to appreciate the centrality of love in the redeeming work of the risen Christ.

Redeeming Love
The three evangelists all yield material for those who appreciate the resurrection of the crucified Jesus, with its aftermath in the outpouring of the Holy Spirit, as the climax of loving salvation

which comes from our gracious God. The radiantly beautiful Angel of the Lord (Matthew 28:3), who acts as a kind of heavenly 'double' for the risen Jesus, reminds us of the connection between beauty, love and redemption. Beauty rouses our love and inspires us to act. We desire and give our hearts to what is good and beautiful. The incomparable divine beauty and goodness already revealed in the risen Christ can trigger our love and so transform our lives. St Augustine of Hippo expressed for all time how the divine beauty works to arouse our love and change our existence (*Confessions*, 3. 6; 9. 4; 10. 27). In Luke's story of the meeting with Jesus on the road to Emmaus, Cleopas and his companion experience how the presence and teaching of the risen Jesus set their 'hearts burning within them' (Luke 24:32) – a further hint of the way in which the beauty and truth of the risen Lord have a transforming impact.

But it is John who sets out even more clearly the redemptive power of divine love at work through the death and resurrection of Jesus. The evangelist has already repeatedly signalled this theme of saving love in the farewell discourses of Jesus and, not least, through an inclusion which links the start of chapter 13 with the close of chapter 17. At the end of his long prayer, Jesus prays that his suffering, dying and rising will bring his followers into the communion of love which is the life of the Trinity (John 17:26). At the beginning of the farewell discourses, John tells us about Jesus: 'Having loved his own who were in the world, he loved them to the end [or uttermost]' (John 13:1).

When we move to the two Easter chapters of John, so many verses can speak to us of the redeeming love deployed by the risen Jesus. The words of Vincent Bruemmer (quoted in the last chapter and again at the head of this chapter) about reciprocal love and our owing our identity as persons to others are wonderfully exemplified in the meeting between Mary Magdalene and her risen Lord. In that encounter we see her lasting identity being bestowed on her through the love which Jesus has for her and through her love for him. Let me dwell rather on the closing chapter of John's Gospel.

Many readers of John notice the theme of Peter's sin and

forgiveness. Three times in the courtyard of the high priest he denies being a disciple of Jesus (John 18:15–27). That sombre episode ends when the cock crows, but without any repentant tears from Peter. After the resurrection he visits the open and empty tomb (John 20:2–10). He is presumably there with the other disciples when Jesus appears, breathes the Holy Spirit into them, and gives them the power to forgive sins (John 20:19–23). Finally, Peter's threefold declaration of love matches his denial of a few days earlier and brings the commission to feed the Lord's lambs and sheep (John 21:15–17).

Beyond question, John's final chapter shows Peter being lovingly forgiven for a recent act of cowardice. But the text says much more about love than that. It shows us the risen Jesus bringing up a buried past, and with loving delicacy healing old memories for Peter *and for the reader*. As so often in John's Gospel, the text invites us to identify with the men and women who meet and experience Jesus. In this case our identification with the disciples in John 21 entails remembering situations into which we have been drawn right from the first chapter of that Gospel. This is an exercise that can recall and heal our own buried past. Let us see how the final chapter of John can lovingly bring about a healing redemption.

After chapter 20 the situation we meet in the final chapter is astonishing. Summoned by Mary Magdalene's unexpected discovery, Peter has visited the empty tomb of Jesus (John 20:3–10). On Easter Sunday evening, along with the other disciples, he 'rejoices' to see the risen Lord, receives the Holy Spirit, and is sent on mission by the risen Jesus (John 20:21–22). Thomas 'called the Twin', who was absent on Easter Sunday evening and expresses his crass doubts about the resurrection, a week later sees the risen Christ and blurts out his confession: 'My Lord and my God' (John 20:24–29). Then we suddenly find Peter, Thomas and five other disciples out fishing, almost as if Jesus had never existed and had never turned their lives around. Peter's announcement, 'I am going fishing' (John 21:3) seems as if he is ignoring or even denying the association with Jesus which has so shaped his very recent past. At the least it suggests deep uncertainty about the future and the way Peter and his fellow disciples should begin their ministry to the world. Nevertheless, the text evokes what we already know, not from John, but from the other Gospels: Peter and 'the sons of Zebedee' (John 21:2) were fishermen when Jesus first called them (Mark 1:16–20). Something of their past is showing through.

John's final chapter opens by stating that it will describe how the risen Jesus manifests himself again to the disciples (John 21:1), his third self-manifestation after the resurrection (John 21:14) – actually his fourth if we include the appearance to Mary Magdalene alone (John 20:11–18). Three times in John 21:1 and 14, we find the verb 'manifest', the same word used to close the story of the changing of water into wine: 'This, the first of his signs, Jesus did at Cana in Galilee, and manifested his glory; and his disciples believed in him' (John 2:11). The narrative encourages the reader to remember that episode by noting that one of the seven fisherman, Nathanael, comes from 'Cana in Galilee' (John 21:2). Once again the past is being recalled. Just as Galilee saw Jesus working his first sign to manifest his glory, so now in the same Galilee the risen Jesus manifests himself as 'the Lord' (John 21:7, 12).

He does so 'just as day is breaking' (John 21:4). He is there on the beach when the dawn comes and darkness slips away. The scene evokes the cure of the blind man (John 9:1–39) and the claim of Jesus: 'I am the light of the world' (John 9:5). The spring dawn at the end of the Gospel can also take the reader back even to the very beginning of the Gospel and the Light which shines in the darkness to enlighten and give life to every man and woman (John 1:4–9). In the closing chapter of John the seven disciples have fished all night without catching anything. Now the stranger on the lakeside tells them to cast their net on the right side of the boat. They do so and make an enormous catch of 153 fish (John 21:6, 8, 11) – a symbol of fullness[4] and an echo of the 'life in abundance' (John 10:10) which the Gospel, right from its prologue, has promised that the Light of the world will bring (John 1:4).

The extraordinary catch of fish, the only such miraculous or

[98]

semi-miraculous event of its kind in the Easter stories of all four Gospels, recalls the multiplication of the loaves *and fishes* (John 6:1–15). In the discourse which follows that sign, Jesus speaks of people being 'hauled' or drawn to him (John 6:44), a verb which turns up later in the promise: 'When I am lifted up from the earth, I will draw [literally 'haul'] all people to myself' (John 12:32). Now in the closing chapter of the fourth Gospel the same verb recurs when Peter 'hauls' ashore the unbroken net containing the 153 fish. Symbolically Peter the fisherman is now engaged in the work of 'hauling' others to the Lord (see Mark 1:17) or gathering 'the scattered children of God' (John 11:52).

The remarkable way in which the net remains unbroken, despite its enclosing so many large fish, can bring to mind the unity of believers promised by Jesus through the image of gathering all into 'one sheepfold' (John 10:16). The images of fish and sheep differ, but the meaning is the same.

When the disciples reach land, they see that Jesus has already prepared for them some fish and bread (John 21:9). In preparing a meal Jesus ('the cook'?) has done something which none of the Gospels ever report him doing during his lifetime. But then with words and gestures that evoke what he has done when multiplying the loaves and fishes (John 6:8–11), Jesus asks the disciples to bring some of the fish which they have just caught (John 21:10). He 'takes' and 'gives' them bread and fish (John 21:13), just as he has done earlier (John 6:13). The reader is being lovingly challenged to recall an earlier story. Once more the text works to summon up a past grace by which we can be touched again.

Many readers link 'the disciple whom Jesus loves' (John 21:7, 20) with the figure repeatedly characterised in this way from the Last Supper in John 13:23 to the visit to the empty tomb in 20:2. Many readers likewise link the 'charcoal fire' (John 21:9) around which the disciples take their breakfast with the charcoal fire in the high priest's courtyard, the scene of Peter's denial (John 18:18, 25). The morning scene on the beach prompts a new evaluation of Peter and ourselves. A broken past can re-surface and be lovingly redeemed.

However, despite the explicit recall of the Last Supper in John 21:20, what may pass unnoticed is the way the lakeside breakfast works to heal the memories of earlier meals in John's narrative. Those earlier meals proved occasions of deadly threats against Jesus (John 12:1–11), disputes about 'wasting' precious nard to anoint the feet of Jesus (John 12:4–8), the betrayal of Jesus (John 13:21–30), and a 'misunderstanding' when the wine ran out during a marriage feast (John 2:3–4). The miraculous feeding of the five thousand (John 6:1–15) is also significant here. It led into a discourse about the bread of life, which ended with many disciples leaving Jesus and the first warning about Judas' treacherous betrayal (John 6:25–71). In a loving and healing way, the Easter breakfast at dawn revokes those earlier meals and the crises associated with them, and promises Jesus' saving presence through the eucharistic meals to come.

Most readers have a sense of what the Gospel is saying through Peter's threefold profession of love (John 21:15–17). Peter must acknowledge and come to terms with his sinful failure. Renouncing his threefold denial (John 18:15–17), he is lovingly forgiven and rehabilitated. Undoubtedly the professions match the denials. But the story conveys a richer sense of healing than just that.

Right from the start of the Gospel, Jesus has put questions to various individuals and groups: 'What are you looking for?' (John 1:38); 'Will you also go away?' (6:67); and so on. The end of the Gospel features the only question Jesus ever repeats, and he puts it three times to Peter: 'Do you love me?' In the closing chapter an old habit returns and is intensified. Peter faces Jesus the loving questioner, from whom he receives forgiveness and a lasting commission.

At their very first meeting Jesus had spoken to Peter as 'Simon, son of John'(John 1:42), an address repeated three times at their last, post-resurrection encounter (John 21:15–17). In the imagery of the Good Shepherd and his sheep, the Good Shepherd calls his sheep by their names (John 10:1–8). Peter is now commissioned to feed the Lord's lambs and sheep. The great catch of fish with which chapter 21 opens might have shaped the missionary charge as 'cast my net, catch my fish'. Yet in John's imagery it is not fishing but shepherding the flock which entails danger and even death (John 10:11–15, 17–18). Peter's commission will call him to martyrdom (John 21:18–19) in the service of the flock. No longer is it a matter of his deciding whether or where to go or stay (John 6:67–68). He will be carried where he does not wish to go (John 21:18–19). Like Philip at the beginning of the Gospel (John 1:43), Peter at the end hears the simple but radical call to faithful discipleship: 'follow me' (John 21:19, 22).

John's narrative shows us Peter recovering his past before he begins the pastoral ministry which will eventually lead to his martyrdom. As we have just seen, the last chapter of John recalls much of Jesus' ministry and story, right back to the very prologue. Peter is taken through all this, down to his shameful failure during the passion. The past is not denied, but recalled, forgiven and lovingly redeemed. A healing through love becomes the basis for Peter's new future.

John 21 begins with Peter going out fishing. He is, as it were, taking time off while he seeks for a pattern of meaning in his life and particularly in his recent experiences. It is almost as if, for the moment at least, the grand design has eluded him. But the Lord appears at dawn to heal Peter's past and enrol him in an heroic mission which will lead to a martyr's death (John 21:18–19).

Something of this redemptive process can also come true for readers of the fourth Gospel. To the extent that they have allowed themselves to become involved with Jesus in the whole of John's story, the final chapter will have its saving effect on them. It will bring up memories of Jesus and past encounters with him, so as to heal and redeem that past. For the readers, no less than for Peter, the 'follow me' of the last chapter can evoke and heal their memories as the basis for a new future.

This way of looking at John 21 accounts for the deeply haunting quality which many readers find in it.[5] Somehow we have heard and experienced it all before. There is an affinity and continuity between our lives and what we read at the end of

John. The closing chapter works to bring back to the surface painful and sinful memories. But they can become the start of a fresh future – through the loving presence of the risen Lord, who is our goal (because we have accepted the 'follow me') and our necessary support.[6]

My final chapter has explored what the Easter narratives of Matthew, Luke and John yield for those who ask: What does the resurrection of the crucified Jesus reveal about God? What does it say about the redemption achieved for us and for our world? In particular, the three evangelists indicate possible approaches to redemption as the victory of life, the reconciliation of sinners and a loving healing of memories. A coherent pattern of deliverance, atonement and transforming love emerges from the Easter texts.

If the heart has its reasons and love enables us to recognise reality, lovers also know that they can never exhaust the truth about the objects of their love. They know that it may be better to say too little than too much. There is a time to fall silent like those friends of Gandalf when the old man unexpectedly returned: 'Between wonder, joy and fear they stood and found no words to say.'[7] Christ's resurrection remains far more than the sum of any or all descriptions of it. At some point we will find no more words to say. Then we can do no more than pay silent homage to the awesome nature of this resurrection from the dead, the beginning of God's new creation.

An Unfinished Postscript

A FINAL RE-READING OF THIS BOOK has raised fresh questions and introduced what seem to be further insights. Reflection on Chapter 1, for instance, recalled how analogies may prove friends or foes of Easter faith. Early comparisons between Christ's resurrection, on the one hand, and such biblical stories as the creation, the exodus from Egypt, and the deliverance of the prophet Jonah, on the other, flourished in the art and worship of Christians who knew their scriptures and experienced how baptism and the eucharist 're-presented' the dying, burial, and rising of Jesus. Modern attempts, however, to find analogies between the appearances of the risen Christ and the experiences of bereaved persons, far from always being motivated by a desire to enhance community worship, seem at times to be aimed at blunting anything once-and-for-all about these appearances and the event which they revealed, Christ's glorious resurrection from the dead. All analogies call for a detailed scrutiny which attends both to similarities and differences. From whatever source they come, only such a scrutiny will discern between those analogies which helpfully illuminate aspects of Easter faith and those which obfuscate it. The list of such illuminating natural, biblical and liturgical analogies outlined in Chapter 1 could be enriched by another set: the present-day experiences of apparently powerless victims whose paradoxical love, joy, freedom and hope lend vivid credibility to the Easter message.[1]

In Chapter 2 and, even more, in Chapter 3, I was beginning to speak as an 'insider' to Easter faith. Beyond question, a unilateral attention to what insiders experience might easily encourage an unreasonable isolationism which, in the spirit of 'I speak only with those who agree with me', refrains from hearing the challenges and criticisms of outsiders and even insists that mounting any rational defence of religious/Easter faith is neither possible nor desirable. Hence not only the first two chapters but also the opening section of Chapter 3 engaged in debate with non-believing outsiders.

In any such dialogue and debate it seems regularly necessary to emphasise that the core issue is believing (or not believing) in Someone whom believers experience as gloriously alive. When believing in a person, we normally can point to good reasons for doing so but not to totally and utterly overwhelming reasons. If that were the case, it would be hard to see how we could freely accept such a relationship of trusting belief. Being simply compelled to accept someone seems incompatible with the freedom needed for interpersonal trust and belief. Hence the kind of 'solid, substantial, objective evidence' imagined by Dan Cohn-Sherbok would rule out the possibility of faith in Jesus:

> If Jesus appeared surrounded by hosts of angels trailing clouds of glory and announcing his Messiahship for all to see, this would certainly be compelling. But it would have to take place in the public domain. Such an event would have to be witnessed by multitudes, photographed, recorded on video cameras, shown on television, and announced in newspapers and magazines worldwide. Jesus' appearance would have to be a global event, televised on CNN and other forms of the world's media. Further, if as a consequence of his arrival, all the prophecies recorded in the scriptures were fulfilled, the ingathering of the exiles, the rebuilding of the Temple, the resurrection of all those who have died, the advent of the Days of the Messiah, final judgement – I would without doubt embrace the Christian message and become a follower of the risen Christ.[2]

Such compelling evidence would seem to rule out, rather than rule in, the possibility of freely becoming a follower of Jesus. Instead it seems to be a scenario of the final coming, when the time of trusting belief will be over and all the world will simply be confronted with the sovereign rule of the risen Christ.

Revisiting Chapter 3 has also reminded me that there is a greatness to Easter claims which no amount of theory can hope to explain. That chapter sought to illustrate how the resurrection is far from being merely an interesting mental exercise. In our personal experience of life and worship, the redeeming power of the risen Christ becomes felt and imaginable.

The debate in that chapter with those like William Clifford, who insist unilaterally on the claims of evidence, can be furthered by introducing some pertinent remarks about 'opinion' and 'belief' made by John Rist. 'We hold opinions,' he observes, 'not merely because they are logically well grounded, but as much because they are familiar to us and, like old friends, have been thus part of us, and we are . . . loath to abandon them.' In other words, 'to hold an opinion is not merely a matter of our ration- ality; it is also a matter of our emotions, our character, our loves'[3] – to which I would add 'and also of our experiences of life and worship'.

When reading Chapter 4, some would have liked more on the historical debate about the empty tomb. What, for instance, should we make of Paul's silence in 1 Corinthians 15:3–5? He reports the tradition that 'Christ died, was buried, has been raised on the third day, and appeared to Cephas [Peter] and to the Twelve.' Does the Apostle's silence about the discovery of the empty tomb imply that he knew nothing about it or even that he dismissed it as of no importance?

What we meet here belongs to the larger question of Paul's 'silence' about many important and historically reliable details: the parables preached by Jesus, his miraculous activity, Jerusalem as the scene of his crucifixion, and so forth. If silence about the discovery of the empty tomb prompts us to reject that tradition, logically we should do the same with the parables of Jesus and so on. But, of course, only a lunatic fringe would do that.

Some use 1 Corinthians 15 somewhat differently in making a case against the empty tomb story. In that chapter Paul struggles to enlighten his readers about the nature of the risen body and says much that applies equally to Christ and to others. Surely, the argument goes, even though we expect a glorious existence to come, our bodies decompose in the grave and so did the body of Jesus? Surely the fact that Paul links our bodily fate with that of Jesus tells against the empty tomb story? However, while undoubtedly developing the link between ourselves and Christ, Paul also indicates that the parallel is by no means complete. He calls the risen Christ 'a life-giving spirit' (1 Corinthians 15:45) – something which does not apply to us. In Romans 4:25 he writes of Christ as 'having been raised for our justification', but Paul never suggests that we have been or will be raised to 'justify' others. In short, while linking our expectations with the crucified and risen Christ, Paul also clearly distinguishes the two cases. He thus leaves space for a resurrection shortly after death which involved the body of Christ which had been laid in the tomb. Paul certainly does not propose a perfect parallel, as if what will happen to us corresponds precisely to what happened to Christ.

As we saw in Chapter 4, in first-century Judaism those who hoped for resurrection, despite all their differences, never expected a personal resurrection in which bodies which had been buried were not involved. No empty tomb meant no resurrection. For these and other reasons, Wolfhart Pannenberg rightly stated that 'for Paul the empty tomb was a self-evident implication of what was said about the resurrection of Jesus.'[4]

Apropos of Paul on the resurrection, many commentators note the connection between the historical affirmation 'he was buried' (1 Corinthians 15:4) and the understanding of baptism as symbolising 'burial with Christ' (Romans 6:3–4). Taken together the two passages fit with the Gospel story of Jesus receiving a dignified burial at the hands of Joseph of Arimathea. Some commentators also push the parallel between the neophyte emerging from the waters of baptism and Christ emerging gloriously alive from his tomb. Perhaps this is correct. But, all in all, a stronger case can be made straight from 1 Corinthians as understood within the Jewish thought-world of the first century: for Paul the resurrection necessarily implied an empty tomb.

Finally, the narrative theology of redemption developed in

Chapter 5 could milk the Gospel of Matthew for further themes. The redemption initiated by the resurrection of the crucified Christ will be not only bodily but also thoroughly social and cosmic. The apocalyptic imagery of earthquakes associated both with the crucifixion and the resurrection (Matthew 27:50–54; 28:2) characterises these events as initiating the end of all things and the general resurrection to come. Matthew drives home this point by writing of the resurrection of 'many saints' on the occasion of Christ's own dying and rising (Matthew 27:52–53). The social and even cosmic nature of redemption comes through clearly. These dimensions of redemption emerge at least as strongly through the 'universalising' language of Christ in the 'Great Commission' with which Matthew closes his Gospel: '*All* authority has been given to me *in heaven and on earth*. Go therefore and make disciples of *all nations*, baptising them in the name of the Father and of the Son and of the Holy Spirit and teaching them to observe *all* that I have commanded you. And behold, I will be with you *all days, even to the end of time*' (Matthew 28:18–20).

This book has reflected on Easter faith, which both reveals the truth about Jesus, God, the world and ourselves and promises to transform our life here and hereafter. The resurrection of the crucified One has created Christian identity and existence, and in fact has shaped for ever the identity and existence of all human beings. It is surpassingly important to know through personal experience the risen Jesus, without whom nothing is truly valuable or lastingly useful (see Philippians 3:8–11). Undoubtedly, Easter faith makes striking demands on believers. Yet any cost can be cheerfully borne. That is because such faith responds to the good news of the risen Christ, as Ludwig Wittgenstein put it, 'believingly – i.e. lovingly'. 'It is *love*,' he continued, 'that believes the Resurrection.'[5]

Notes

Chapter 1: Are Background Theories Decisive?

1. G. Luedemann, *The Resurrection of Jesus: History, Experience, Theology,* trans. J. Bowden (Minneapolis: Fortress Press, 1994).

2. Ibid., pp. 6, 14–15, 19, 69, 178, 211; see my review in *Gregorianum* 77 (1996), pp. 357–9.

3. See T. Nagel, *The View from Nowhere* (Oxford: Oxford University Press, 1985); and A. G. Padgett, 'Advice for Religious Historians: On the Myth of a Purely Historical Jesus', in S. Davis, D. Kendall and G. O'Collins (eds.), *The Resurrection* (Oxford: Oxford University Press, 1997), pp. 287–307.

4. See P. Gwynne, 'Why Some Still Doubt That Jesus' Body Was Raised', in D. Kendall and S. Davis (eds.), *The Convergence of Theology* (Mahwah, NJ: Paulist Press, 2001), pp. 355–67.

5. G. Luedemann, 'The Resurrection of Jesus: The Greatest Hoax in History', *Forum* 10 (1994), pp. 161–75, at pp. 162–65, 168; id., *What Really Happened to Jesus?* (London: SCM Press, 1995), pp. 135–7; id., *The Resurrection of Jesus,* pp. 180–81.

6. A. J. M. Wedderburn, *Beyond Resurrection* (London: SCM Press, 1999), pp. 220–26.

7. Ibid., pp. 217–18.

8. Ibid., p. 220.

9. W. Marxsen, *The Resurrection of Jesus of Nazareth* (London: SCM Press, 1970), pp. 150–54.

10. Ibid., pp. 22–3, 30, 110, 118, 119. One must admire the strict tenacity with which Marxsen follows through on his position and with breathtaking understatement can brush the resurrection aside as 'a somewhat unusual event'.

11. See C. A. J. Coady, *Testimony: A Philosophical Study* (Oxford: Clarendon Press, 1992), pp. 179–98.

12. On further analogies to the resurrection of Jesus, see G. O'Collins, 'The Risen Jesus: Analogies and Presence', in S. E. Porter et al. (eds.), *Resurrection* (Sheffield: Sheffield Academic Press, 1999), pp. 195–217, at pp. 197–9.

13. J. Hick, *The Metaphor of God Incarnate* (London: SCM Press, 1993), pp. 24–6.

14. W. Dewi Rees, 'The Hallucinations of Widowhood', *British Medical Journal* (2 October 1971), pp. 37–41; references to this article will be given intra-textually. 'Hallucination' is, as P. H. Wiebe points out, 'a theory-laden expression. It might appear to be straightforwardly descriptive, but . . . it conceals many assumptions about what is real and what humans are capable of knowing.' (P. H. Wiebe, *Visions of Jesus* [New York: Oxford University Press, 1997], p. 195).

15. A. M. Greeley, *Religion as Poetry* (New Brunswick: Transaction Publishers, 1996), pp. 217–27.

16. There are two minor qualifications (about Peter and Paul) to be made here. First, according to Luke, Peter, some years after his foundational vision (1 Corinthians 15:5; Luke 24:34), once heard (but did not see) the risen Lord (Acts 10:14; 11:8). Secondly, Paul reports some words he heard from the risen Lord (2 Corinthians 12:9) years after his foundational vision (1 Corinthians 15:8). Probably drawing on Pauline traditions but composing the stories to fit his theological and literary purposes, Luke tells of two visions by night and one vision by day (Acts 18:9–10; 22: 17–21; 23:11). These visions come after the Damascus Road encounter and do not match that foundational episode when the risen Lord appeared to him without Paul reporting any words being said (1 Corinthians 9:1; 15:8) – not least because they do not establish for Paul the risen existence of Christ and because the emphasis is all on what the Lord says to him in some critical situations.

17. Luedemann, *The Resurrection of Jesus*, pp. 99, 225, n. 398.

18. C. Murray Parkes, *Bereavement Studies of Grief in Adult Life* (London: Routledge, 3rd edn, 1996).

19. Luedemann, *The Resurrection of Jesus*, pp. 97–100. We can trace Strauss' explanation for the Easter appearances even back to the second-century attack on Christianity by Celsus. He accounted for St Peter's experience of the risen Christ by saying that, 'just as has happened to very many, he translated into reality the object of his desire' (Origen, *Contra Celsum*, 2.55).

20. For a bibliography and summary account of various views see J. D. G. Dunn, 'Christ Mysticism', *The Theology of Paul the Apostle* (Grand Rapids, Michigan: Eerdmans, 1998), pp. 390–96.

21. For an introductory account and extensive bibliography see 'Mysticism, Mystical Theology', in F. L. Cross and E. A. Livingstone, *Oxford Dictionary of the Christian Church* (Oxford: Oxford University Press, 3rd edn, 1997), pp. 1127–28; see the cautionary remarks by D. Turner, 'Mysticism', in A. Hastings et al. (eds.), *Oxford Companion to Christian Thought* (Oxford: Oxford University Press, 2000), pp. 460–62.

22. According to Luke, when Paul returned to Jerusalem after his Damascus Road encounter, he was praying in the Temple and 'in ecstasy' he 'saw

Jesus telling' him to 'leave Jerusalem quickly' (Acts 22:17). This sub-sequent episode, which confirmed Paul's vocation to the Gentiles, involved a trance in which Luke stressed the commissioning of Paul rather than any seeing and so followed a pattern frequently found in the Old Testament: 'in a vision the Lord said' to so and so.

23. K. Rahner, *Foundations of Christian Faith: An Introduction to the Idea of Christianity* (New York: Seabury Press, 1978), pp. 276–77. In earlier publications Rahner had discussed the experiences of Christian mystics and visionaries and criteria for distinguishing authentic experiences from hallucinations; see his *Visions and Prophecies* (New York: Herder and Herder, 1963).

24. G. O'Collins and D. Kendall, 'The Uniqueness of the Easter Appearances', *Focus on Jesus* (Leominster: Gracewing, 1996), pp. 111–27; this is an abbreviated version of an article with the same title which appeared in *Catholic Biblical Quarterly* 54 (1992), pp. 287–307.

25. Rahner, *Foundations of Christian Faith*, pp. 276–7.

26. Even if it mentions 'visions and revelations [both plural] of the Lord', 2 Corinthians 12:1–4 does not report that anyone was glimpsed or anything seen. In recalling an out-of-the-body experience which took the form of a heavenly journey (not his foundational encounter in the AD 30s with the risen Jesus but some subsequent experience in the AD 40s), Paul speaks rather of things which were 'heard' and which 'no mortal is permitted to repeat'. Nothing was seen and any revelatory message which he heard remained private and was not communicated for others.

27. Rahner, *Foundations of Christian Faith*, p. 274.

28. Wiebe, *Visions of Jesus*, especially pp. 40–88.

29. Ibid., p. 89.

30. Ibid., p. 145.

31. Some writers have introduced further analogies by comparing the Easter appearances to Old Testament theophanies or to Christian experiences of the Holy Spirit. Both analogies have their serious limits: on the former see O'Collins and Kendall, *Focus on Jesus*, pp. 113–15, and G. O'Collins, *Jesus Risen* (Mahwah, NJ: Paulist Press, 1987), pp. 91–4; on the latter see G. O'Collins, *Retrieving Fundamental Theology* (Mahwah, NJ: Paulist Press, 1993), pp. 142–7.

Chapter 2: Historical Evidence and Its Limits

1. My correspondent could be defended for insisting that the resurrection involves a claim not only about what has already happened to Jesus but also about what will happen to the cosmos when the world process will be completed at the *eschaton*. We are obviously not in a position to 'discover and describe' the definitive shape of things to come. But did my correspondent want to allege something which is quite different and very dubious,

a complete discontinuity between the whole of human history and the final condition of all creation?

2. W. Pannenberg, *Jesus-God and Man* (London: SCM Press, 1968), p. 99; italics mine.

3. Ibid., p. 89.

4. Ibid., p. 100.

5. Ibid., pp. 99, 113; trans. corrected.

6. Ibid. p. 98.

7. R. Bultmann, *Theology of the New Testament*, vol. 1 (London: SCM Press, 1965), p. 26.

8. W. Herrmann, *The Communion of the Christian with God* (London: Williams and Norgate, 1906), p. 76.

9. Pannenberg, *Jesus-God and Man*, pp. 67, 83–8.

10. Ibid., p. 107.

11. G. O'Collins, *Fundamental Theology* (Mahwah, NJ: Paulist Press, 1981), pp. 131–3, 145–50. This interplay between knowing, loving and hoping is a basic principle in G. O'Collins and M. Farrugia, *Catholicism* (Oxford: Oxford University Press, 2003). On love and knowledge see G. O'Collins and D. Kendall, *The Bible for Theology* (Mahwah, NJ: Paulist Press, 1997), pp. 65–6.

12. Kant's three questions at the end of his *Critique of Pure Reason* help to place the three distinguishable but inseparable dimensions of faith, even if it would be preferable to move them away from individualism, give them a Jesus-orientation, and make them read: 'What can we know of Jesus? What ought we to do about Jesus? What may we hope for from Jesus?'

13. G. E. Lessing, *Historical Writings*, selected and trans. H. Chadwick (Stanford, Calif.: Stanford University Press, 1967), p. 53.

14. In ancient Christianity Augustine of Hippo and others developed this line of argument: see G. O'Collins, 'Augustine on the Resurrection', in F. LeMoine and C. Kleinhenz (eds.), *Saint Augustine the Bishop* (New York: Garland, 1994),pp. 65–75, esp. pp. 67–9.

15. C. F. Evans, *Resurrection and the New Testament* (London: SCM Press, 1970), p. 132.

16. N. T. Wright, 'Jesus' Resurrection and Christian Origins', *Gregorianum* 83 (2002), pp. 615–35.

17. See Pannenberg, *Jesus-God and Man*, p. 96.

18. For the basic data about Enoch and Elijah, see R. S. Hess, 'Enoch', *Anchor Bible Dictionary*, vol. 2 (New York: Doubleday, 1992), p. 508; J. T. Walsh, 'Elijah', ibid., pp. 463–6.

19. See R. Swinburne, 'Evidence for the Resurrection', in S. Davis, D. Kendall, and G. O'Collins (eds.), *The Resurrection* (Oxford: Oxford University Press, 1997), pp. 191–212, esp. pp. 207–12. Despite his doubts, Wedderburn presents well this argument about the reason for Christians making Sunday

their day of worship (A. J. M. Wedderburn, *Beyond Resurrection* [London: SCM Press, 1999], pp. 48–50). Both Swinburne and Wedderburn draw on the classic study by W. Rordorf, *Sunday: The history of the day of rest and worship in the earliest centuries of the Christian Church* (London: SCM Press, 1968).

20. See G. Luedemann, *The Resurrection of Jesus: History, Experience, Theology*, trans. J. Bowden (Minneapolis: Fortress, 1994), pp 80–84, 97–100.

21. See Chapter 1, n. 19.

22. See H. Küng, *On Being a Christian* (London: Collins, 1976), p. 364.

23. See J. Jeremias, *Jerusalem in the Time of Jesus* (London: SCM Press, 1969), pp. 374–5.

24. See P. F. Carnley, *The Structure of Resurrection Belief* (Oxford: Clarendon Press, 1987), p. 60.

25. See A. Yarbro Collins, 'The Empty Tomb in the Gospel According to Mark', in E. Stump and T. P. Flint (eds.), *Hermes and Athena* (Notre Dame, Ind.: University of Notre Dame Press, 1993), pp. 107–40, at pp. 130–31; see my 'The Resurrection: The State of the Questions', in Davis, Kendall and O'Collins, *The Resurrection*, pp. 5–28, at pp. 15–17. In *The Homeric Epics and the Gospel of Mark* (New Haven: Yale University Press, 2000), D. R. MacDonald argues that Mark wrote a fictional narrative in imitation of Homer's epic poetry. As Stephen Davis points out (in a paper to be published in *Books and Culture*), if Mark wanted his readers to understand Jesus 'as a hero like but greater than Ulysses', the evangelist managed to disguise his intentions extremely well. 'After all,' Davis remarks, 'neither Luke nor Matthew, who obviously paid close, word-for-word attention to the text of Mark, notice any Homeric influence. Neither did any of the Easter Church Fathers, several of whom were exceedingly well versed in the Greek classics, and were at pains to demonstrate the superiority of the Bible to those works. Neither did *anybody* until MacDonald came along centuries after the fact . . . it is puzzling that Mark hid his intentions as well as MacDonald says he did. Why didn't Mark occasionally *mention* Homer or *quote* from Homer or *use Homeric vocabulary* or make direct *allusions* to Homer? This is the way we usually show that a given text depends upon an earlier one. And Mark is not at all shy about quoting from or alluding to the Hebrew Bible . . . it remains a major challenge to MacDonald to explain why the influence of Homer was not noticed until the twenty-first century.'

26. See e.g. my *Jesus Risen* (Mahwah, NJ: Paulist, 1987), pp. 112–27.

Chapter 3: Testimony and Experience

1. Here, as often in this book, 'evidence' refers to non-personal evidence. In the case of witnesses, we can speak of their 'giving evidence', and then

'evidence' refers to personal testimony. The context should make it clear whether 'evidence' is being used in a personal or a non-personal way.

2. W. K. Clifford, 'The Ethics of Belief', in W. Kaufmann (ed.), *Religion from Tolstoy to Camus* (New York: Harper, 1961), pp. 201–20, at p. 206; hereafter references will be given intratextually.

3. Ibid., pp. 221–38, at p. 231; hereafter references will be given intra-textually.

4. See M. Larmer, *Water into Wine* (Montreal: McGill, 1988); id. (ed.), *Questions of Miracle* (Montreal: McGill, 1996); R. Swinburne, *The Concept of Miracle* (London: Macmillan, 1970); id. (ed.), *Miracles* (London: Collier Macmillan, 1989). Along with the issue of the resurrection and miracles, one would need to deal with the largely godless views of Hume and Clifford. For his part, Clifford assures us that nature is uniform: 'no evidence, therefore, can justify us in believing the truth of a statement which is contrary to, or outside of, the uniformity of nature' (Clifford, 'The Ethics of Belief', p. 219). Obviously then no evidence could ever justify accepting the resurrection of the dead Jesus, since such an event is clearly outside, if not contrary to, the uniformity of nature.

5. See C. A. J. Coady, *Testimony: A Philosophical Study* (Oxford: Clarendon Press, 1994).

6. See J. Bowden, 'Resurrection in Music', in S. Barton and G. Stanton (eds.), *Resurrection* (London: SPCK, 1994), pp. 188–97.

7. See D. A. Hagner, *Matthew 14–28*, Word Biblical Commentary , vol. 33b (Dallas: Word Books, 1995), p. 533; C. S. Keener, *A Commentary on the Gospel of Matthew* (Grand Rapids, Mich: Eerdmans, 1999), pp. 455–6.

8. See Blaise Pascal (1623–62), 'He [Christ] is in agony till the end of the world'; *Pensée*, no. 552 in the standard editions, but no. 919 in the order of *Pensées* as Pascal left them at his death.

9. Sobrino reports the 'learning' experiences of those who came to help in El Salvador; see J. Sobrino, *Christ the Liberator* (Maryknoll, NY: Orbis, 2001), pp. 71–2.

10. See P. F. Carnley, *The Structure of Resurrection Belief* (Oxford: Clarendon Press, 1987), especially pp. 266–368.

11. See C. F. Davis, *The Evidential Force of Religious Experience* (Oxford: Oxford University Press, 1989).

Chapter 4: The Empty Tomb of Jesus: History and Theology

1. The 'we' of 'we do not know' (John 20:2) may indicate that Mary Magdalene was not alone, even though the text names only her.

2. See A. Yarbro Collins, *The Beginnings of the Gospel. Probings of Mark in Context* (Minneapolis: Fortress Press, 1992), pp. 134–8.

3. See R. Pesch, *Das Markusevangelium*, vol. 2 (Freiburg: Herder, 1977), pp. 519–28.

4. See his 1937 remark quoted at the head of this chapter, from *Culture and Value*, trans. P. Winch (Oxford: Basil Blackwell, 1980), 33C.

5. While agreeing (against Yarbro Collins) that Mark used an earlier tradition in composing his empty tomb narrative, Francis J. Moloney argues that at least in one important point Mark 'subverted' (i.e. deliberately changed) the common tradition about women finding the tomb of Jesus to be empty and then announcing the Easter message to the male disciples. Driven by a theological agenda that wanted to picture *all* the disciples, men *and* women, as having finally failed, Mark changed the tradition and wrote of the women's fearful flight and disobedient silence (Mark 16:8). See F. Moloney, *The Gospel of Mark: A Commentary* (Peabody, Mass.: Hendrickson, 2002), p. 344, n. 26. We examine below the thesis of universal 'final failure' proposed by Moloney and some others before him; see my *Interpreting the Resurrection* (New York: Paulist Press, 1988), pp 53–67, 80–83.

6. Danove, P. L., *The End of Mark's Story: A Methodological Study* (Leiden: E. J. Brill, 1993).

7. See my *Jesus Risen* (London: Darton, Longman and Todd, 1987), pp. 124–5.

8. See G. Stemberger, *Der Leib der Auferstehung. Studien zur Anthropologie und Eschatologie des palaestinischen Judentums im neutestamentlichen Zeitalter (ca. 170 v.Chr.-100 n. Chr)* (Analecta Biblica 56; Rome: Biblical Institute Press, 1972); G. O'Collins, 'The Resurrection: The State of the Questions', in S. Davis, D. Kendall and G. O'Collins (eds.), *The Resurrection* (Oxford: Oxford University Press, 1997), pp. 5–28, at p. 20.

9. See Moloney, *The Gospel of Mark*, p. 344; O'Collins, *Jesus Risen*, p. 126.

10. See The Constitution on Divine Revelation (*Dei Verbum*) of November 1965, nos. 2, 4, 14, 17; see G. O'Collins, *Retrieving Fundamental Theology* (Mahwah, NJ: Paulist Press, 1993), p. 54.

11. T. Dwyer, *The Motif of Wonder in the Gospel of Mark*, JSNT Supplement (Sheffield: Sheffield Academic Press, 1996); in the present paragraph references to this book will be given intratextually.

12. J. L. Magness, *Sense and Absence. Structure and Suspension in the Ending of Mark's Gospel* (Atlanta: Scholars Press, 1986), pp. 100–101.

13. Dwyer, *The Motif of Wonder*, p. 192. When interpreting the women's silent flight as their failure, Moloney does not enter into debate with Dwyer. In 'A Rhetorical Analysis of Mark's Construction of Discipleship', in S. E. Porter and D. L. Stamps (eds.), *Rhetorical Criticism and the Bible* (Sheffield: Sheffield Academic Press, 2002), P. L. Danove also interprets the 'fear' in Mark 16:8 negatively, (Danove, *The End of Mark's Story*, pp. 289–91). He too does so without any reference to Dwyer's study, which had appeared two years before the 1998 conference from which Danove's chapter came.

14. In Acts 13:32, Luke emphasises the revelatory importance of the resurrection in disclosing the paternity of God and the sonship of Christ. He applies

to the event of the resurrection the psalmist's words about the Davidic king's sonship manifested on the day of his installation: 'You are my son. Today I have begotten you' (Ps 2:7).

15. I realise that some exegetes might react with suspicion to the idea that, like other texts, the concluding chapter of Mark can mean and communicate to its readers more than its author ever consciously meant. Of course, we should reject interpretations which are contrary to what the evangelist wished to express. But, provided that does not take place, we should recognise how the meanings of his and other texts, when read in new contexts by later readers, can go beyond the original authors' intentions when they wrote in particular situations for specific audiences. See the coda at the end of this chapter.

16. On the inter-dependence of giving and receiving love, see John Rist, *Real Ethics* (Cambridge: Cambridge University Press, 2002), p. 109.

17. V. Bruemmer, *The Model of Love: A Study in Philosophical Theology* (Cambridge: Cambridge University Press, 1993), p. 171.

18. See C. Harrison, *Beauty and Revelation in the Thought of Saint Augustine* (Oxford: Clarendon Press, 1992).

19. On this verse see D. A. Hagner, *Matthew 14–28*, Word Biblical Commentary, vol. 33b (Dallas: Word Books, 1995), p. 789; C. S. Keener, *A Commentary on the Gospel of Matthew* (Grand Rapids, Mich: Eerdmans, 1999), pp. 643–4.

20. A. J. Close, 'Is Cervantes still joking?', *Times Literary Supplement,* 12 July 2002, p. 3.

21. On issues of meaning and the original authors' intentions, see H. G. Gadamer, *Truth and Method* (rev. ed., London: Sheed and Ward, 1989); G. O'Collins, *Fundamental Theology* (rev. ed., Mahwah, NJ: Paulist Press, 1986), pp. 251–9; G. O'Collins and D. Kendall, *The Bible for Theology* (Mahwah, NJ: Paulist Press, 1997); The Pontifical Biblical Commission, *The Interpretation of the Bible in the Church* (Vatican City: Libreria Editrice Vaticana, 1993); P. Ricoeur, *The Conflict of Interpretations: Essays in Hermeneutics* (Evanston: Northwestern University Press, 1974); id., *Interpretation Theory: Discourse and the Surplus of Meaning* (Fort Worth: Texas University Christian Press, 1976); O. Rush, *The Reception of Doctrine* (Rome: Gregorian University Press, 1997); A. C. Thiselton, *New Horizons in Hermeneutics* (London: HarperCollins, 1992).

Chapter 5: Easter As Revelation and Redemption: Matthew, Luke and John

1. C. F. Evans, *Resurrection and the New Testament* (London: SCM Press, 1970), p. 84. This section contains several characteristic Matthean motifs: 'making disciples', the teaching aspect of the Church's mission, Jesus' instructions which communicate the new law, the mission to 'all nations' prefigured by

the names of gentile women in Jesus' genealogy (Matthew 1:1–17) and the visit of the Magi (Matthew 2:1–12), and his enduring presence which the Angel of the Lord had anticipated in the birth narrative (Matthew 1:23). D. A. Hagner comments on Matthew 28:18–20: 'It is very clear that the words [of Jesus] are recast in Matthew's style and vocabulary . . . This fact, however, does not amount to a demonstration that Matthew composed the passage *ex nihilo* . . . He may simply have worked over and re-presented a tradition available to him' (*Matthew 14–28*, vol. 33b [Dallas: Word Books, 1995], p. 883).

2. Curiously such large commentaries as D. L. Bock, *Luke, Volume 2: 9: 51–24: 53* (Grand Rapids, Mich.: Baker Books, 1996), J. A. Fitzmyer, *The Gospel according to Luke X–XXIV*, Anchor Bible 28a (Garden City, NY: Doubleday, 1985) and J. Nolland, *Luke 18: 35–24: 53*, Word Biblical Commentary 35c (Dallas: Word Books, 1993) have little to say about Luke's important Easter theme of 'life'.

3. The two angelic figures in Acts 1:10–11 who 'explain' the ascension belong with the similar figures in Luke 24:4–7 in constituting the angelic 'inclusion'.

4. Greek zoologists, it seems, reckoned that there were 153 different kinds of fish; thus the catch of John 21 symbolises that with the help of Jesus the disciples have caught 'all kinds'; for details see R. Schnackenburg, *The Gospel According to John*, vol. 3 (London and Tunbridge Wells: Burns and Oates, 1982), p. 357.

5. This way of approaching the message of John's last chapter makes me regret the title chosen by Schnackenburg, 'The Problems thrown up by John 21', in ibid., pp. 341–74. Instead of expounding its spiritual riches, this great biblical scholar seems more concerned to demonstrate that John 21 is an 'editorial conclusion' and not a 'postscript, appendix or epilogue'. I owe much more to the way Rowan Williams expounds John 21 in his *Resurrection: Interpreting the Easter Gospel* (London: Darton, Longman and Todd, 2002).

6. Some observations which John Rist makes converge with the redemptive love embodied in John 21. 'Only love,' Rist writes, 'could induce us to take responsibility for our past; yet without taking that responsibility we cannot complete a *single* "narrative" of our own life' (*Real Ethics* [Cambridge: Cambridge University Press, 2002], p. 108). I have suggested that by the power of his love the risen Christ encourages Peter to take responsibility for his past. Thus the Apostle can move beyond his divided self and eventually – through martyrdom – complete the single narrative of his life. The love of the risen Christ, I would add, can also have a similar impact on the readers of John's Gospel; they too are called to complete the single narrative of their lives.

7. J. R. R. Tolkien, *The Lord of the Rings*, II, *The Two Towers* (London: George Allen and Unwin, 1954), p. 98.

An Unfinished Postscript

1. See J. Sobrino, *Christ the Liberator* (Maryknoll, NY: Orbis, 2001), pp. 71–3.
2. 'The Resurrection of Jesus: A Jewish View', in G. D'Costa (ed.), *Resurrection Reconsidered* (Oxford: Oneworld, 1996), pp. 184–200, at p. 198.
3. J. Rist, *Real Ethics* (Cambridge: Cambridge University Press, 2002), p. 103.
4. W. Pannenberg, *Systematic Theology*, vol. 2 (Edinburgh: T. & T. Clark, 1994), p. 359; see my *Christology* (Oxford: Oxford University Press, 1995), pp. 94–5.
5. L. Wittgenstein, *Culture and Value*, trans. P. Winch (Oxford: Basil Blackwell, 1980), 32c, 33c.

Select Bibliography

Some Modern Studies

Avis, P. (ed.), *The Resurrection of Jesus Christ* (London: Darton, Longman and Todd, 1993).

Barton, S. and Stanton, G. (eds.), *Resurrection* (London: SPCK, 1994).

Brown, R. E., *The Virginal Conception and the Bodily Resurrection of Jesus* (New York: Paulist Press, 1973).

Carnley, P. F., *The Structure of Resurrection Belief* (Oxford: Clarendon, 1987).

Catchpole, D., *Resurrection People: Studies in the Resurrection Narratives of the Gospels* (London: Darton, Longman and Todd, 2000).

Davis, S. T., *Risen Indeed: Making Sense of the Resurrection* (London: SPCK, 1993).

Davis, S. T., Kendall, D., and O'Collins, G. (eds.), *The Resurrection* (Oxford: Oxford University Press, 1997).

D'Costa, G. (ed.), *Resurrection Reconsidered* (Oxford: Oneworld, 1996).

Evans, C. F., *Resurrection and the New Testament* (London: SCM Press, 1970).

Fuller, R. H., *The Formation of the Resurrection Narratives* (London: SPCK, 1972).

Greenacre, R. and Haselock, J., *The Sacrament of Easter* (Leominster: Gracewing, 1995).

Heil, J. P., *The Death and Resurrection of Jesus* (Minneapolis: Fortress, 1991).

Keener, C. S., *A Commentary on the Gospel of Matthew* (Grand Rapids, Mich: Eerdmans, 1999), pp. 697–721.

Kessler, H., *La risurrezione di Gesù Cristo* (Brescia: Queriniana, 1999).

Léon-Dufour, X., *Resurrection and the Message of Easter* (London: Geoffrey Chapman, 1974).

Moule, C. F. D. (ed.), *The Significance of the Message of the Resurrection for Faith in Jesus Christ* (London: SCM Press, 1968).

Osborne, K., *The Resurrection of Jesus* (Mahwah, NJ: Paulist Press, 1997).

Pannenberg, W., *Systematic Theology*, vol. 2 (Edinburgh: T. & T. Clark, 1994), pp. 343–72.

—*Systematic Theology*, vol. 3 (Edinburgh: T. & T. Clark, 1998), pp. 375–80, pp. 555–646.

Perkins, P., *Resurrection* (London: Geoffrey Chapman, 1984).

Rahner, K., *Foundations of Christian Faith* (New York: Seabury, 1978), pp. 264–85.

Sobrino, J., *Christ the Liberator* (Maryknoll, NY: Orbis, 2001), pp. 11–110.

Swinburne, R., *The Resurrection of God Incarnate* (Oxford: Oxford University Press, 2003).

Thiselton, A. C., *The First Epistle to the Corinthians* (Carlisle: Paternoster, 2000), pp. 1169–1313.

Williams, R., 'Resurrection,' in A. Hastings *et al.* (eds.), *The Oxford Companion to Christian Thought* (Oxford: Oxford University Press, 2000), pp. 616–18.

——*Resurrection: Interpreting the Easter Gospel* (London: Darton, Longman and Todd, 2002).

Wright, N. T. *The Resurrection of the Son of God* (London: SPCK, 2003).

Some Works by Gerald O'Collins on the Resurrection

(These are listed chronologically; further articles, reviews and chapters in books which deal with the resurrection can be found in the complete bibliography provided by D. Kendall and S. T. Davis (eds.), *The Convergence of Theology: A Festschrift Honoring Gerald O'Collins, s.j.* [Mahwah, NJ: Paulist Press, 2001], pp. 370–98.)

Books

The Easter Jesus (London: Darton, Longman and Todd, 1973; new edn. 1980); published as *The Resurrection of Jesus Christ* (Valley Forge, Pa: Judson Press, 1973).

What Are They Saying about the Resurrection? (New York: Paulist Press, 1978).

Jesus Risen (Mahwah, NJ/London: Paulist Press/Darton, Longman and Todd, 1987).

Interpreting the Resurrection (Mahwah, NJ: Paulist Press, 1988).

The Resurrection of Jesus Christ: Some Contemporary Issues (Milwaukee: Marquette University Press, 1993).

Articles and Chapters in Books

'Newman's Seven Notes: The Case of the Resurrection', in I. Ker and A. G. Hill (eds.), *Newman After a Hundred Years* (Oxford: Clarendon Press, 1990), 337–52.

'The Uniqueness of the Easter Appearances' (with D. Kendall), *Catholic Biblical Quarterly* 54 (1992), 287–307.

'Resurrection', in A. E. McGrath (ed.), *The Blackwell Encyclopedia of Modern Thought* (Oxford: Blackwell, 1993), pp. 553–57.

'Augustine on the Resurrection', in F. LeMoine and C. Kleinhenz (eds.), *Saint Augustine the Bishop* (New York/London: Garland, 1994), pp. 65–75.

'On Reissuing Venturini' (with D. Kendall), *Gregorianum* 75 (1994), pp. 153–75.

'The Resurrection: The State of the Questions', in S. T. Davis, D. Kendall and G. O'Collins (eds.), *The Resurrection* (Oxford: Oxford University Press, 1997), p. 5–28.

'The Resurrection of Jesus: The Debate Continued', *Gregorianum* 81 (2000), pp. 589–98.

Index of Names

[121]